Abel Polese

The SCOPUS Diaries and the (il)logics of Academic Survival

A Short Guide to Design your Own Strategy And Survive
Bibliometrics, Conferences, And Unreal Expectations
in Academia

Abel Polese

THE SCOPUS DIARIES AND THE (IL)LOGICS OF ACADEMIC SURVIVAL

A Short Guide to Design Your Own Strategy And Survive
Bibliometrics, Conferences, And Unreal Expectations
in Academia

ibidem-Verlag
Stuttgart

Bibliografische Information der Deutschen Nationalbibliothek
Die Deutsche Nationalbibliothek verzeichnet diese Publikation in der Deutschen Nationalbibliografie; detaillierte bibliografische Daten sind im Internet über http://dnb.d-nb.de abrufbar.

Bibliographic information published by the Deutsche Nationalbibliothek
Die Deutsche Nationalbibliothek lists this publication in the Deutsche Nationalbibliografie; detailed bibliographic data are available in the Internet at http://dnb.d-nb.de.

All icons in this book are made by Freepik from www.flaticon.com.

∞

Gedruckt auf alterungsbeständigem, säurefreien Papier
Printed on acid-free paper

ISBN-13: 978-3-8382-1199-2

© *ibidem*-Verlag
Stuttgart 2018

Contents

Foreword
On what criteria build, and develop, an academic career, and one's reputation, and how this book was conceived

> "Their genuine goal would be to measure academic performance through quality so to acknowledge individuality and creativity of each intellectual. But if you measure quality through (quantitative) indicators, then academics are just numbers."
> (during a conversation with Artem...)

For some time already, academics from a number of regions of the world, and from virtually all disciplines, have been put under increasing pressure to publish in Scopus, or Web of Science-indexed journals. "Is it a good thing or a bad thing?" I was asked during a workshop.

It is neither. I see it as the result of a long change in the higher education sector that has been happening for some time now. Once upon a time, universities were such a scarcely populated world that you did not necessarily need a PhD to be hired as a lecturer, there was little necessity to ask who was better than whom. Scholars would be known because of an authoritative article, or book in a certain discipline. It was another world back then, a world that I like to imagine romantically slow, with less travel and CO_2 emissions and where word of mouth had functions that have been taken over, at least partly, by the Internet now. It was generally assumed that academics were somehow more educated than the others and thus, almost automatically produced smart and quality outputs.

What happened that changed this idyllic scenario? Well, the scenario could be idyllic for teachers but not necessarily for students or people who wanted to enroll in a university but did not manage to for a number of reasons. Much has changed and there are other places more indicated to explore the developments of the university sector. However, in a nutshell, one can observe two tendencies. One is the democratization of higher education, and thus the idea that it should be available to virtually everyone wishing to enhance their qualifications. The other is the demand for university degrees to gain competitiveness in the labor market, and this is a global tendency.

With a demand exponentially growing, the supply has quickly adapted, and the university sector has radically changed. The number of universities across the globe has increased, as well as the variety of formative offers, leading to new degrees and majors that did not exist before. An even faster growth has been witnessed in fields that are perceived as landing you into a good job relatively quickly after completion of a degree. Likewise, the demand for degrees from universities that are perceived as "the best ones" has grown.

This also means that the capacity, or at least potential, of universities to generate money has significantly increased to various degrees, depending on the country and the discipline concerned. More visible and prestigious universities are in high demand and can basically impose their own standards, prices, conditions. The lower you go on the "prestige scale" the more difficult this becomes but, as a general tendency, the university sector interacts with, and affects a growing number of actors, nationally and internationally.

In spite of this, general perceptions of the university sector seem to suggest that money for research, and the higher education sector, has shrunk. Indeed, I often hear from colleagues that funding for universities has decreased but this is a tricky statement. My general impression, since there are a variety of tendencies across world regions or even within the same country, is that the percentage of public funding for universities has decreased. In fact, public expenditure for universities in some cases has increased. However, if the number of universities in a country grows, then the fraction of the money allocated to each university, on average, decreases. Likewise, if the number of universities stays the same but they become bigger, to accommodate more students—and therefore they need more teachers and administrators, their budgets become larger and the fraction of budget that can be paid by public funds gets smaller.

This tendency does not necessarily mean bad times for universities, or at least not all of them. Those able to differentiate income sources, or simply to find a good channel for revenues, may live better than before. But in general, the sector changes and so do the rules of the game so a number of actors find themselves in a transition period, say dire straits, until they find a new way of generating a stable income and a new equilibrium.

When resources become scarce, they have to be distributed with more care within the sector, but also within the same university, faculty and department. While there might be a number of criteria to use for competition, the main official one used at this stage is "academic quality" broadly defined. Money (and so power and prestige) goes to universities, faculties, departments, scholars who deserve it measured through a basket of academic performance standards. This can include teaching, research output and other criteria used to assess a university. However, in reality, it comes down to a few items amongst which research performance is, in my view, the main one.

When someone needs to decide where to enroll, in addition to the question, "What would I like to study," an important question a prospective student (or their parents) will ask is, "What are you going to do after you finish?" Universities, and disciplines, that will give you better labor market perspectives will be targeted more intensively than others. However, perception on how a degree will affect your performance in the job market is largely influenced by the prestige of a university, which is often resulting from its ranking in research performance such as its visibility in the media or by the number of Nobel Prizes winners teaching there, regardless of how good the teachers are, or how often they are replaced by their assistants because they are traveling the world to present at conferences here and there.

Of the two main criteria used to allocate funds, thus, one is research performance and the other, at least partly, is an indirect result of research performance.

Research performance becomes thus crucial at the macro (which universities to fund more) and micro (which department, or scholar, to support more) levels. When funders need to agree on criteria to decide whether to give money to this or that university, to that or this discipline, they will look at the "quality" of research outputs. Universities, or disciplines, that deliver "better quality," or that have more impact on the society, deserve more money. But how to objectively measure quality? And also, what happens with the universities, or disciplines, that do not make it into the hall of fame of state-funded universities?

The quest for academic quality and the Scopus fetish

How to measure quality? As a general rule you need a controller or evaluator, a benchmark and some indicators, be these qualitative or quantitative. However, at the pace the higher education sector is developing quality control is indeed a challenge. Academia was born as a small circle of people working on things that were unintelligible for the rest of the world. Controlling quality was more of a basic exercise, done by word of mouth, perceptions and a number of simpler criteria than we have now. However, quality control in a community where you know virtually everyone by their name is easier than controlling quality in an imagined community of several hundred thousand academics, even more if there is an expectation that a single standard can be theoretically applied to all disciplines.

There are, of course, widely accepted qualitative criteria such as being awarded a Nobel prize, national scientific awards and other kinds of acknowledgements. But this is for a restricted minority of academics that distinguish themselves and bring a visible and tangible contribution to the world. What about the others (common mortals and non-Nobel prize winners)? And what about these disciplines whose contributions to the world are crucial but not so visible and, let alone, tangible? Philosophy helps people to think and be critical but there is no Nobel prize for philosophy or a proper job market for philosophy graduates.

We are talking here about a situation where we have to measure the output of masses (more educated but still academic masses) and find a reason to say "A is better than B."

In many cases, the answer has been one: Scopus (or Web of Science, most of the logic I use to understand Scopus here can be applied to Web of Science).

Scopus is a scientific database of academic journals that are, at least officially, peer-reviewed and that deliver the highest scientific quality in the world. Until recent times, the only database available was Thomson and Reuters Web of Science (WoS but also known as ISI). Scopus has, however, gained consensus among a number of circles for being more inclusive and has filled a niche that ISI had left, for some reason, uncovered. Humanities and Social Science journals are under-represented in the ISI database if compared to Scopus. As a result, a number of national authorities have turned to Scopus, or use Scopus in conjunction with ISI, as the indicator of quality as a complementary database to measure the quality of academic outputs.

The principle is simple: if a journal is in Scopus, it means it has passed a quality examination. This allows us to pledge that future publications in a given journal are likely to keep a similar scientific standard and thus be of good quality. If a scientist publishes in a Scopus-indexed journal, it is reasonable to assume that their output is of good quality. The better a journal is ranked in Scopus the higher the (alleged) quality of its article. Therefore, if you publish in a top journal (according to Scopus rankings), you are publishing a top article. This is an assumption endorsed sometimes without even reading the article.

The immediate and logic response of countries wishing to enhance their scientific profile has been simple: they have asked their scientists to prioritize Scopus journals. This may be acceptable for younger scholars who are growing up with this myth and can be defined as the "Scopus generation." But what about the scholars who have not prioritized Scopus for 20 or 30 years, constructing a career on other principles? How to redirect your career choices in the short delays that you are given by your national authorities?

Second, and perhaps more important: Scopus is certainly an excellent attempt to classify quality in academic production but is more likely to produce fetishes than career advice. The career of an academic, their reputation and their satisfaction cannot possibly depend solely on Scopus articles. There are journals that are not in the database but that everybody from your field reads. Shall we stop targeting these ones at once to devote time to Scopus articles? Science is also made of dissemination activities and sometimes a non-academic article is likely to bring more attention than an academic article. Further in this direction, Scopus is a database for journals. What about a book or book chapters that count close to nothing in some countries now? Shall we, at once, stop writing chapters? In some cases, a chapter is a contribution to a collective book that may contribute to significant advancements of scientific knowledge. In many other cases, it is a way to be part of a team, to work with people you have always wanted to work with, to work under an editor who is one of your references in your field. If my academic guru invites me to contribute to a volume edited by a first-class publisher, shall I respond, "Sorry, it's not in Scopus?" Also, think about the situation where you are asked to contribute an article to a young academic journal that is committed to quality, innovation and is in line with the way you see scientific progress. It is likely that the journal is not (yet) in Scopus but needs to survive, develop and gain credibility. You have a moral choice now: to do what you are asked to do or to do what you believe in? Many people mention working in academia to be able to keep a certain degree of freedom. But if Scopus becomes your main fetish, is this real freedom?

As a friend commented when reading this book, "only dead fish go with the flow." Make your own choice but remember one thing: academia was born to produce people who are capable to think autonomously and contribute to shaping the world, rather than being shaped by bureaucratic rules.

How much is too much?
What this book is about and about a life-career balance

This is a book exploring academic career strategies. I have conceived it as answers to questions that have been in the air for a while and to which only standard (and politically correct) answers have been available so far.

My goal is to help you to think of your own career strategy while remaining healthy in your mind. This, in spite of the zillions of things that you are supposed to do to get academic recognition. However, instead of telling you what you should be doing, I will provide you with a cost-benefit analysis of some of the available choices, or ways to carry out the tasks that you are supposed to engage in and most of the things you are supposed to do to enhance your academic careers.

We all know that academics need to publish, and peer review, articles; they need to look for funding, attend conferences, establish collaborations, engage with public dissemination activities. But how much is too much? What is the amount of effort one should put into each of these activities? What is the ideal input-output ratio? How much should you work for an article? Are 5 articles a year a good target? Shall you try to publish in the No.-1 journal in the world in your discipline or are middle-range journals enough?

The obvious answer is that only you are in the position of assessing this and that all of this depends on your attitude, and motivation, to complete a given duty. Only you can know how much time, nerves, efforts and sleep deprivation you need to complete a given task. Only you know how much stress you can handle. Hence, your main task is not to publish a given article but to remain healthy in your mind, or at least to avoid burnout, so to be able to keep on working, and publishing, more over the space of several years.

We are constantly under pressure from a variety of directions. Our university, our ministry or other quality-controlling institutions, our line manager. We also have other obligations: towards colleagues inviting us to participate in projects, towards that nice journal editor that is leading a project we like so much, towards those nice people who paid for our travel and accommodation for that great conference at a hotel near the beach and are now trying to pull together a collected volume to which they kindly ask you to contribute to, even if publishing with them will bring no benefits to your career. A general understanding of academia is that, in the payback for the limited amount of money you can earn (with some exceptions) is a degree of freedom that other jobs do not grant you, it grants you a lot of freedom and allows you to do what you would like to do. But how many of us take advantage of this freedom?

Eventually, academic careers are stressful not because of the pressure you get from your line manager but because of the pressure you put on yourself. Because of targets, often unrealistic or overambitious, that you set for yourself willingly, all the times that you say yes to an invitation, and from the frustration, you get for not meeting your objectives that seemed realistic when you chose them.

Much has been written about what one has to do to progress their academic career. My problem with these approaches is that it simply puts extra pressure on emerging academics who are parachuted into "you should do this, this and this," without revealing the hidden (and sometimes dark) mechanisms behind a number of practices. Failing to understand a dynamic, to grasp some of the open secrets of academia, can delay your work, or even make a task impossible to complete. This book is an attempt to look with a critical, and sometimes cynical, eye at the elements considered crucial to academic careers but on which we often get standard, and standardized answers. For instance, sessions on "How to publish in a peer-reviewed journal," usually consist of suggestions on how a standard, or a good, reviewer would look at your article. My problem with this is that things rarely happen in the standardized way they are described. There is much distortion in a peer-review process: reviewers are usually late, some of them criticize you destructively, the journal gets too many submissions to deal properly with your article and you might end up with useless comments accompanied by a rejection letter some twelve months after submitting. You do it all right, according to the books, and it goes all wrong. How would you cope with that? How would you avoid this situation?

To think strategically of your career, at least in my view, means to become aware of the most common distortions in academia (in what way things could "go wrong") and act accordingly to deliver what you are expected to deliver. Ultimately, strategy for me refers to the capacity to identify a compromise between what you are expected, or requested, to do and what you would like to do, what would make you happy or at least content. This involves, the capacity to take risks and do things for which you will receive no money, or formal recognition from your employer, but because you feel you will gain something else from it. Personal satisfaction, friendship, extra time for yourself or your family, sleeping are also part of your career inasmuch as they allow you to better concentrate on what you do and do it with love. You could work less and work better if you understand what it is really worth working for and investing time in. But, to do this, you should be able to discern what you have to do to survive, and thus to keep your job, and what you think you need to do but in fact is not mandatory or bringing anything into your professional development at this stage, so you would be better off skipping it, at least this time.

How to read, and use, this book

I assume that most readers will be academics, or people familiar with academia and its standards in terms of references, style and format. Well, this is not an academic book but a book about how to strategically think about your academic career. You can, of course, read it from the beginning to the end but you can also pick any question (or topic) you find interesting and start reading from there. Then move backwards, then forward, until you do not need it anymore or simply get tired of us (the book and me).

I have divided the book into the following sections that are, in my view, some of the most important aspects around which one needs to think about one's academic career:

- o **Writing** deals with the actual process of writing and the approaches you might want to use to write something that becomes easily readable by people from your academic community.
- o **Publishing** is the further logical step to writing but in a different world. It explains why "good" articles may get rejected while "less good" articles may effortlessly make it into a journal quite easily.
- o **Growing** explores the way you can boost your profile and move from a junior to a more senior academic status.
- o **Shining** acknowledges the existence of two distinct processes. One is the production of a written or other kinds of work. The other is the efforts that you need to make it known and become visible and appreciated as an academic.
- o **Niching** highlights the fact that you cannot always be famous everywhere but need to identify, and conquer, your public. To do this you need to become aware of your selling points and use them to come to occupy a given place in the academic "Olympus".
- o **Networking** acknowledges the fact that you will not be able to advance much in your career by simply sitting in your library, or lab, and writing about your results. You also need to connect with people, start collaborations and engage with stakeholders.
- o **Funding** singles out possible strategies to deal with fundraising activities, a thing that is increasingly required when you are an academic and deciding whether you really want to do that and how to, just in case.

Each section hosts a number of questions (or topics) about which I share my experience and position. I have tried to develop each topic, and its answer, within the space of about one A4 page. However, some topics are inevitably longer. Each question is self-standing in that you do not need to have read any other questions to understand the answer. Some topics are mentioned more than once and answers are provided in more than one section. This was done when I thought that a question could be answered from different angles and that each angle could help you understand one aspect of a given topic. For instance, publishing can be used to grow professionally, or to network but with other ends and an answer encompassing all the possible implications of publishing would be too complex, or long.

I have no reason to hide that, during my career, I have mostly mingled with scholars from the social sciences, broadly defined. After a first degree in economics, I completed an M.A. in European studies and a Ph.D. in anthropology. I have no experience in publishing in science journals or in patenting new discoveries. But in my free time, I read biology, genetics and psychology. I have also been a Scottish Crucible Fellow and a Global Young Academy member. Both organizations select scientists from many disciplines to consider research, and science, as one, not as composed of many disciplines. They suggest, and I believe, that research policy is one and that scientists have a lot to win if they unite, regardless of their discipline, when seeking a dialogue with funding and policy institutions, as well as with the general public. Thanks to these experiences, I have had the chance to work, back to back, with chemists, nutritionists, ICT, biologists, medical doctors and colleagues from other disciplines, who have shaped the approach I developed in this book.

I suggest here that, although some dynamics might change across different disciplines, and countries, the mechanisms behind the publishing industry, and the long-term goals of each scientist, are very alike:

o To keep doing research and progress in career.
o To have some kind of impact on the academic community, and possibly society.
o To balance work-related activities and personal life.

How each of us does it depends on our own strategy. And so, it is the balance between the above three goals. Ultimately, some scholars might sacrifice one or more aspects to work on other ones at some stage of their career. Some short-term goals might emerge at some point for personal ambitions (i.e., become famous, make more money) and means of achieving an objective might differ, depending on the strategy one chooses.

In addition to one's objectives, the must do of an academic is very alike cross countries, regions and disciplines. We all work in a given environment that is shaped by the goals and values of the institution we work for and we are all regularly evaluated by national authorities controlling academic performance of our institutions. What is required from us is, therefore, simple at its basic level:

- o To carry out quality research and publish in the best possible journals (where the definition of the best possible journal changes depending on where you work).
- o To contribute to teaching activities depending on your position and role in the team you are integrated into.
- o To engage in a set of professional service activities. This cluster is the most unclear one since it mostly depends on the position of your national evaluation institutions on a number of activities. It also depends on the ambitions of your university, and department. I have thus tried to elaborate on what I thought were the most common ones.

As a result, my claim here is that this book can be useful to scholars from a wide array of disciplines, and approaches, who want to reflect on their career, on what they do, on how they do it, and get a different view on the dynamics of the academic world. As a friend said, most of the things written in this book are known intuitively by most scholars. However, I took time to systematize this knowledge, add my personal experience, and reflect on the meaning of what we do, why we do it in a certain way and whether it could be done in a different one.

Acknowledgements

The core idea of this book was developed during a 3-day workshop on academic publishing strategies at the Regional Studies Center in Yerevan, which the Academic Swiss Caucasus Network generously provided funding for. The workshop, organized by my friend Mikail Zolyan, was recorded and then transcribed into a long document that remained forgotten on my computer for some time. A further boost of the idea came when I was asked to deliver a series of lectures for the Social Innovation Lab at the Mykolas Romeris University in Vilnius, and I have to thank Andrius Puksas, who offered to invite me using a grant from the Lithuanian visiting professor funding scheme.

In an effort to find a topic that was not already available, and thus offer the students something new, I came to develop daily workshops based on the topics that have built this book. A further series of seminars on publication strategies was organized by my friend Amiya Kumar Das at Tezpur University and permitted me to reflect further on the idea.

However, the turning point was a talk at Vinnitsa Medical University, organized by my good friend and colleague Tetiana Stepurko in 2016. After the lecture, Oleg Vlasenko, the local vice-rector for research approached me and gently asked for a copy of my book, the book that I had just presented at his university.

There was no such book in my list of publications, or even in my pipeline. But there could be one. I went back to the original transcripts to make the document more readable. The initial idea was to do some basic editing and then publish it. The advice contained in these pages had been praised by most participants from my workshops, so I thought that minimal editing was needed. However, the more I was doing this the more I realized that, to have a better impact, I had to de-contextualize the examples, widen the public I was talking to, take more cases from my professional life, and publish it in the form of a manual.

This was tremendously boosted by the positive and enthusiastic response I received from Chris Schoen at ibidem Verlag. He was positive from the very first interaction and, which was extremely important for me, agreed to sell the book at the minimal possible price, making it affordable for virtually anyone. He even granted his permission that some parts could be kept available online for free, a thing that increases the visibility of the project and allows undecided people to read it and then decide whether they want to buy it.

The number of books, and initiatives, on academic strategy, is growing. However, apart from freely available blog posts and conferences, most books I have seen on how to live your academic career are sold at exorbitant prices. What is the point of targeting a public of young scholars, or scholars from lower performance regions, since they are less likely to get exposed to such knowledge, and then sell at a price they could not afford? I believe a great advantage of this book is its affordability and my main goal is that people, and colleagues, learn to navigate the system a bit better.

The people mentioned above have had a direct impact on the life of this book. They have been all extremely useful, at various degrees and in various moments. Some of them have shown me "their way" of doing things and made me discover that there are not two but many ways of dealing with the same issues equally successfully. Some others have provided me with feedback, formally or informally, during workshops, discussions or on the various drafts of the manuscript. However, for having shared with me anecdotes, stories, episodes, frustrations that made us laugh and reflect on the dark, and twisted, sides of academia, and of human nature in general I wish to express my gratitude to also the people below, mentioned in a random sequence since I cannot think of any criteria to rank them (and I am a chaotic person anyway):

Michael Gentile, Hyun Bang Shin, Gul Berna Ozcan, Alena Ledeneva, Donnacha Ó Beacháin, Andrea Graziosi, Vanni D'Alessio, Jeremy Morris, Peter Rutland, John Doyle, Rico Isaacs, Eileen Connelly, Rustam Urinboyev, Tetiana Stepurko, Oleg Vlasenko, Andrius Puskas, Mikael Zolyan, Elena Darjania, Maria Kazakova, Klavs Sedlenieks, Ketevan Kutsushvili, Arnis Sauka, Nicolas De Pedro, Christian Giordano, Nicholas Hayoz, Marcello Mollica, Rob Kevlihan, Amiya Kumar Das, Licinia Simao, Filippo Menga, Raquel Freire, Karolina Stefanczek, Stefano Braghiroli, Rajan Kumar, Adrian Fauve, Vika Akchurina, Alessandra Russo, Francesco Strazzari, Stefano Bianchini, Rodica Ianole, Diana Lezhava, Erhan Dogan, Bruno De Cordier, Heiko Pleines, Ilona Baumane, Denis Volkov, Soso Salukvadze, Rajan Kumar, Erhan Dogan, Filippo Menga, Gina Mzourek, Ruth Neiland, Colin Williams, Giorgio Comai, Valerie Lange, Florian Bölter.

Eventually, this book results not only from my academic reflections but from conversations, and strategic thinking, that arose also when performing non-academic tasks and talking with entrepreneurs, NGO workers, civil servants and whoever I have crossed paths with to share an opinion, a cup of tea, or simply freely talk about life. The number and variety of people who have inspired me informally are so wide that I prefer not to thank anyone in particular. Those who have regularly discussed strategy with me at the four corners of the world know it and I know it. It is to them also that I owe the way my attitude and mindsets have been shaped and many of the reflections you will find in the next pages.

I also wish to thank:

The participants of all the various workshops that have provided this book with their feedback, critical engagement with my words, or simply for patiently listening to what I wanted to share.

The notorious Reviewer 2. We all know why.

Dublin City University's Faculty of Humanities and Social Sciences' Book Publication Scheme through which I received partial financial support to finalize this book.

My children, who are sitting next to me on this plane while I complete this introduction and claim not to know what strategy, or this book, is about. But who have become highly sophisticated strategic thinkers whenever they want to get something they think they need, or simply want and I have been learning from them as well.

Anyone who has despised, offended, betrayed, criticized unconditionally, patronized, attacked, or silently hated me; who has talked behind my back or tried to stab me in the back (fortunately, only allegorically so far). You have acted as great motivators to reflect on my own mistakes, my attitude in certain situations, on why some things did not work the way I wanted and, in general, on my life and career strategy. Sometimes I have blamed myself for ending up in such situations, more often I have understood that your problem was not me but in yourself. I am grateful for every worry, frustration, deception (well, fortunately not that many, but enough to reflect upon) that I have had to face and live through.

I do not think there are bad people but only bad moments and periods that eventually prompt people to act in ways that they might one day regret. I dedicate this book to all the people I have interacted with in the course of my career, regardless of whether the interaction has left me with a sweet or bitter taste. If I am where I am, it is because of these experiences that I have eventually digested. If anyone has ever hurt me in our interactions, that was meant to happen, and I am happy to give a special mention to any face that I remember behind my (fortunately few) bleak moments. I also hope that this book will prompt a reflection on their career and life and that they can eventually find a way to outlive whatever hardship they have been going through and that made them behave, at a certain stage of their life, in a way that did not necessarily match my values and what I believe in.

Without the negative experience that I have lived with you, I would not have been motivated enough to transform my professional life into a book that is half strategic half autobiographic and that has permitted me to reflect on who I am and where I want to go next.

Bangkok, August 2018

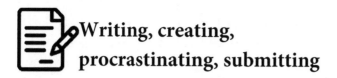# Writing, creating, procrastinating, submitting

The greatest open secret of academia: on the fundamental role of abstracts

Abstracts are possibly the most important detail in the academic world. In many respects, your capacity to express, in a succinct, clear and dynamic manner an idea might determine the place you will occupy in academia. Eventually, a good portion of academic work is devoted to writing, or selecting, abstracts for books, conferences, special issues of journals, workshops, or even funding. Your capacity to convince people who are selecting abstracts that you are worth their attention is, thus, vital.

It is true that acceptance of an abstract is not a guarantee that your final product will be taken. But it may be regarded as a kind of first step towards it. Think about trying to enter some exclusive club. Being properly dressed will allow you to get in, meet people, and eventually play out your skills to try and get what you want. That might not be sufficient, and you might come out of the club empty-handed. However, wearing an inappropriate outfit will definitely leave you out of the club and with no chances to get what you want.

How to write the perfect abstract is a complex question, and I mean with that that the answer can be divided into many little bits, each addressing a different attitude or aspect of abstract submission. These points eventually led me to create a session that I called "the perfect abstract," that I will try to synthesize here.

I regularly solicit, and receive, abstracts from people I have never seen, and I need to decide what stays "in" and what stays "out." By selecting an abstract, I am also making a choice to work (or not) with its author, which is sometimes an important one because, if the author of the abstract is a pain, you will have to endure that pain until the end of the project (or until you kick them out of the project for some reason, but even this takes a lot of effort and nerves).

How important is personal attitude in an abstract? Sometimes a lot, sometimes less. It depends on the kind of activity you are selecting your abstract for. Here we have what, according to my experience, are the most common options.

In a small workshop, a group of 15–30 scholars agree to sit in the same room for 1–2 days and work together on a topic, on a theme. The level of interaction is relatively high here. First, organizers will communicate directly with participants to arrange technical issues (help with accommodation and logistics), circulate papers and agree on sessions. Second, by spending days and social moments together, participants interact formally and informally, contribute to discussions, debates, and possibly argue on academic issues.

The impact of participants with low social skills, or who are simply socially inadequate is high. Think about what the result would be if some of your participants attacked (academically) a speaker during a session. If you are planning a social and networking dinner together, what will happen at the table where more awkward participants are sitting?

Besides, the impact of low-quality presentations and papers is high, given the low number of presentations. All participants will possibly listen to those presentations, and three weak papers out of 15 are almost 20% of the presentations, possibly leading some to conclude that the selection was not properly made.

By contrast, when selecting abstracts for a larger conference the impact of bad papers or unsocial scholars is much lower. If we are talking about an event attracting several thousand presentations, chances are that sessions are parallel, and people will flow to those to hear the most famous scholars. I am not implying that famous scholars cannot deliver bad presentations, or all have good social skills. But if you like the works of a given scholar, you will be more tolerant towards their misdeeds than if you listen to someone for the first time. A famous scholar can deliver a bad presentation without being considered of low quality whereas it is easier to label someone as "bad" whom you hear for the first time and do not like.

You will also suffer less from selecting people with low social skills since most things will be done through a platform or a management tool and one-to-one interaction is reduced. If these people are selected for a section or a panel that you are chairing, social skills of your participants are important.

But a panel lasts usually 1.5–2 hours, after which the group can just disperse or, at least, you can choose whom to take to a networking dinner.

When you deal with young scholars or regional conference, especially if you are working in a region with lower academic productivity or simply different academic traditions, you might allow a bit more margin. What might sound like low social skills might simply be attitudes translated directly from another culture and language that are perfectly acceptable in a given context but in English sound odd or rude. Young scholars have a grace period during which you can assume they are learning and there is sufficient room for improvement to cut them a bit more slack. Yet, since we are not talking about little children (a "young" scholar is still an adult, say 25–35 years old) if I see that someone displays a destructive, or even childish, attitude I will put some extra care in the selection process. The same can be said for quality. If you are working with a region that is trying to develop their academic sector, then you might want to be careful who you select as you are somehow deciding who will be given a further chance for development or not.

For an edited project (a collective book, a special issue of a journal) both quality and social skills are crucial. Not only might you want to deliver something that people will actually read and appreciate, but you are also committing to interacting with a given person over a period of time. You want communication to be clear, that authors take criticisms positively and understand them, that they deliver more or less on time and are willing— and able—to improve their paper. Finally, you also want to avoid someone attacking you because they do not agree with your feedback or management procedures. Disagreement is a part of life, and arguments are a vital part of academia. But it is unpleasant to spend your time literally fighting with someone who is excessively outspoken or aggressive in their communication.

You will have to read abstracts also when acting as a grant evaluator. There is no foreseen interaction with the author of the abstract in this case, but you will be requested to choose what projects to evaluate and poorly written abstracts are usually followed by poorly written projects, painful and harder to assess than good ones.

Why are my abstracts regularly turned down?

Given the above, selection of an abstract might be something more complex than it looks. You might not want to select for your conference someone with poor communication skills or someone who is going to attack someone else while presenting. Just as you might not want to include in your book an author who is always late, unable to take criticism or writes in bad English. You need the maximum amount of details to understand what risks you would be taking by choosing a given scholar for the task you have in mind.

My screening thus starts by looking at the message that I have received from that person. An e-mail already tells me a lot about the attitude and communication skills of the author. If someone is not able to address themselves to me properly and is hoping to attend my conference, how can I endorse them with delivering a presentation that I can expect people will like?

When you sell something, the first rule is to genuinely believe that, by selling that thing, you will improve the life of your customer. Likewise, when I organize a conference or edit a special issue, I need to believe that that author will bring some added value to the product that I am contributing to design and that I am going to sell (academically speaking). Of course, what I need and what I want to offer depends on the final product I am working on. When organizing a small workshop, I need to make sure people will like one another since we will be all working together for a couple of days and I want a pleasant environment. Think of a small event like a party. You do not want to mix the wrong people together or someone will end up unhappy, and you will end up running here and there all the time to solve problems that you would not have had to face, had you carried out a more careful selection process. If I am responsible for a conference with 1000 speakers, I can be less selective. After all, when there are many of them, speakers will split into smaller groups and people who are alike will find one another without my intervention. So, chances are that pedantic participants will find other pedantic ones and happily spend time together.

There might be some other criteria applied when turning down an abstract. For instance, you have limited space in a workshop and have to be more selective; the book you are editing is intended to have a large geographical or disciplinary focus and you can only choose one of the five authors who suggested a similar focus. But my rule is that I will always fight to keep in someone I believe in and if I believe in someone depends on the quality of their abstract. However, with an "abstract" I do not mean 300 words tossed in a Word document. The "perfect abstract" for me has a much broader meaning.

The perfect abstract I: addressing

In business writing courses, one of the first things you learn is, "The package is as important as its content." In other words, the content of a well-formatted document, where you can sense harmony and flow, is already more likely to be considered better than the one from a messy document. This does not apply to writing only. Ask people to compare two kinds of wines, one that costs €10 per glass, but it is taken from a carton, and one that costs €3, but it is an excellent wine taken from an expensive bottle and see how many people will prefer the first one.[1]

You will often tend to think better of authors sending a tidy abstract, even more if it is nicely written, regardless of its content. Just the layout, the division of paragraphs and in general the way the document looks, sometimes gives an impression that in many cases is difficult to forget. Conference abstracts follow the same rule but, conversely from what one might think, an abstract starts in the e-mail to which the abstract is attached.

The first thing you might want to get right is how to address the right person in the right way. If there is a name of the responsible person to which abstracts should be sent, you use this name. This is also a way to show that you have done your homework and know where you are sending your abstract. If I do not see any particular name but a committee and a general address, then I just write "Good morning," "Dear Colleagues/Organizers," "Dear Selection Committee Members," or "To Whom it May Concern."

There are many ways. The important thing is to be personal and use a register proper to the situation. We are in academia, if you write, "Yo, brother, this is my abstract," you are already socially inadequate. What can I expect from someone who is not able to address a colleague properly in a

---

[1] There are many of these experiments in psychology and behavioral economics and I am grateful to Dan Ariel's works, and in particular his book "Predictably Irrational" (http://danariely.com/books/predictably-irrational/) for illuminating me on the topic.

formal occasion? In English, it is usually acceptable to write Dear and then a name or "Dear Dr./Prof. X" if you want to sound more formal. A form of kindness may be to add "if I may" in your first message so you write "Dear Jon (if I may)" and see the response. If the person signs with Dr John X, then you go back to formal communication, if they respond by "Dear (your name)," then you can continue with this tone. You can also write just the name of the person then followed by a comma, which I also like. However, inasmuch as international communication happens in English on a number of occasions, national settings may still shape the perception of the person. The English-speaking world tends to be more easygoing but, for instance, when corresponding with German colleagues, you should be aware that they might want to be a bit more formal, at least in the beginning. For one thing, the Dr. title can be added to your documents and bank cards and becomes, de facto, part of your name. The fact that you become, for official occasions "Mr. Dr." or "Ms. Dr." tells a lot about the importance of a title in your everyday life there.

If you are writing a follow-up email after having met someone and having spoken for some time, my guess would be that it is fine just to use their first name. What I and—probably—most academics dislike is that when someone writes "Dear Mr. Polese," I rarely use my title, so I do not mind at all being addressed as Abel but, if you want to be formal with me, then use my title. If I have spent years trying to get it and then I lose it all of sudden it feels like I am being downgraded all of sudden for no particular reason.

But true that in some cultures Ms. or Mr. is the standard. For instance in France, for some reason, everyone is Monsieur, Madame regardless of the academic title. Dealing with a French academic that has little experience with the English-speaking world can be embarrassing, according to my experience at least, since it takes some time before you can (virtually) agree on salutations and tones of emails.

The perfect abstract II: sending (and receiving) a message

Back to our introductory email, much can be understood from the message and its attachments. In my ideal world a perfect abstract is sent in an email that has the following features:

Subject line: (name of authors) abstract for (name of the event applied for). To understand the importance of the subject line, think of your reaction when you receive an empty subject line by a person (and address) you do not know. Or when you receive an email called "abstract." If each applicant had the same idea, you would have 150 emails with the same title. By the same token, think if someone writes "abstract for the conference" (or, worse, for the event) and you are organizing 3 events (or editing 3 books) at the same time. You will need to write them back and ask for which event, or book, the abstract was sent. Finally, a subject line with the name of the sender, or the recipient's name, sounds like a scam to me and I would rather expect to find some kind of offer of several million dollars from some faraway country. I might just delete it or not notice it.

The body of the message: in an ideal world it would be a short message in the line of "Please find herewith my abstract." I sometimes add, "I would be grateful if you could acknowledge a receipt of this document," just to make sure that my email has not ended into the organizers' junk folder. By contrast, what would you think of someone who sent an empty message with an abstract (it happens more often than one might think)? Or someone writing a long introduction of themselves in the body of the message. I personally find it abusive, in that someone is abusing my time availability: I am going to read your abstract when I have time. If you write a lot in the body of the message, I will have to at least screen it to ensure that it does not contain any vital information that I might be missing. Then, if I simply find that you are explaining to me how qualified you are for this conference or book, I will most likely think that you are showing off. First, if you are a specialist on the topic, let your abstract talk for you. Second, if you want to share something, you are welcome to write before sending the abstract and negotiate, or at least discuss, the topic.

Attachments: if you are requested to send an abstract, it is of little use to send your PhD thesis, MA transcripts or any other documents. I was recently doing a selection for a summer school and a candidate sent me 20 documents. Whilst applicants were requested to only send an abstract, this person sent me a CV, recommendation letters, certificates, degrees, broadcasts, his picture and possibly his family picture too. He put so much care into sending so many documents that, in the end, the only document missing was the abstract itself. Even if the abstract is there, you do not want to dig into piles of documents to find it. I have to confess that my attitude towards someone will not improve because I see how qualified they are. Sometimes you ask for a short biographical statement and receive a photo-reportage. What would you think of the applicant in such case? Do not send any unsolicited documents, unless you really have a reason to do that and, in such case, warn the organizers that the extra document will help them to understand the special situation you are in.

The perfect abstract III: what you want to see in the abstract? (we finally got there)

I receive some abstracts in the body of an email. Guess what I have to do then? Select the text, copy it, open a Word document, paste it, then find the name of the author and contacts, add them, think of a name for the file, save it. It takes 2–3 minutes but if 20 participants do it then I lose an hour of my work. It also requires a higher amount of concentration than just save a document mechanically, which is what you do when there is an attachment.

In other words, by outsourcing some small amount of work to me you are likely to lead me to the conclusion that you lack attention to detail, lack respect or, at best, are just not sufficiently motivated to prepare a document for someone, and this happens even before I read your abstract.

Once I open your document, this is what I would like to find, in an ideal world:

Name of the event you want to attend (or project you expect to join). In 80% of the cases I do not need this, but there is always a chance that I am working on several projects at the same time and by looking at your document I will immediately know where to save it.

Name of the authors and at least one email address so I do not have to go back to your original email to write to you. I think it pays to add your academic affiliation. First, if I can locate you geographically, I can already have an idea on whether I can make a place for you, especially if you are the only one coming from a region or if you are from a university located in a remote area and I want to allow participation from all possible corners of the world.

You might want to add **a short biographical statement** even if it is not required (2–3 lines are fine, more is too much). This might help me appreciate you beyond your abstract. What I would like to understand from your biography is your level of experience and where you work for several reasons. First, I am more open to accept a weaker (although not weak) abstract if someone is from a minor university and I think I can offer them the chance to discuss their research in a setting that is not usual for them. By the same token, I would be a bit more reluctant to accept a weaker abstract from someone coming from a top university. But that is just my position. Other researchers might feel intimidated and accept any abstract from someone coming from a major institution just because they want to populate the workshop with people from top universities.

For instance, if I think the abstract is weaker than the others, but I see the author is from a region with limited scientific achievements, I will read it more carefully and try to read between the lines if the author might have some interesting material. In that case, limited presentation skills might be due to lack of training, or English proficiency. By contrast, I am more likely to reject an abstract if I find it weak and if the authors are from a top university since my assumption is that they have access to a number of opportunities and feedback mechanisms allowing them to write a good abstract already from their early career stages.

Title of the abstract. Believe it or not, I sometimes receive abstracts with no title, which means I cannot refer to it by its name when selecting but also, I wonder why the author has not added it (They forgot? They think it does not matter?).

The abstract (finally!).

The file in the attachment should be named in a way that makes it unique and easy to archive. If everybody names it with the name of the event, I will have dozens of files with the same name. You might just want to call the file your surname and the name of the event. Since I will most likely save abstracts under the name of the authors, when an author does that for me, it saves me a few seconds, but I already start feeling grateful towards them.

The perfect abstract IV: 300 words that will change your life

In my ideal world, the perfect abstract is composed of 4 elements:

- ○ Goal of the paper
- ○ Debates
- ○ Methodology
- ○ Conclusion

It sounds straightforward, but it is not. In my experience, only a very small fraction of abstracts that I have examined meets, even loosely, these criteria.

Goal of the paper: an abstract is not always drawn from a research project that has been completed. Data might be preliminary and even when they are final, you might not have had the time to reflect on their significance. Besides, large conferences are usually organized 1–2 years in advance, so it is perfectly fine to send an abstract with your research still ongoing but assuming that you will have final results by the time of the presentation.

An academic article is usually argumentative so that some reviewers see the verbs "to explore," "to investigate," "to analyze" sometimes as inadequate. By contrast, an abstract can have, as a goal, to explore a correlation, a relationship, and/or a phenomenon, especially if it is based on ongoing or planned research. By all means, however, it may be formulated in an argumentative way "this paper demonstrates (or argues)."

Debates: regardless of whether your goal is descriptive or argumentative, your research approach has been based on a number of hypotheses and located in a number of debates. It becomes easier for the reviewer, especially if they are not 100% familiar with your discipline, to appreciate the significance of your research when you contextualize it. It becomes therefore crucial to explain from which debates you are building your argument or based on what previous studies, hypotheses, results, you are planning to produce and process your empirical data.

Methodology: the methodological section of a paper might need a substantial amount of words, or explanation. There is no need to attempt to fit it into a short abstract, but you might at least mention whether you worked with primary or secondary data, the size of your sample. You could specify whether you conducted a few experiments or interviews but very in-depth ones or collected a large amount of data and to what extent you want to claim representativeness of your sample and for which population.

Conclusion: to what your results (preliminary or final) point to? This could be one line and your abstract might already be strong without it since the goal of the paper is already stated in the section above. But it is like a nice dessert after a meal, a nice way to say goodbye to your reader.

There is no need to use the order I gave above. If the abstract starts with methodology, by the time my brain realizes that the goal of the paper might be missing I have already read to the point where I will find the goal of the paper. The only case where I will be disappointed is when the section I expect to see is actually missing from your 300-word text.

I have seen in a number of blogs using the template provided by PhD comics and I have to admit that it is very close to a perfect abstract.[2]

The image was conceived as a joke but, in spite of its mocking tone, it ticks off all of the boxes: 1) there is space for an argument; 2) it mentions a methodology; 3) it leaves room to add where the argument can be found in current debates and 4) what is the implication for the research. In the end, if you manage, you need four sentences: one to explain the relevance of your research, one to illustrate what you are proposing to do, one to mention your methodology and one to explain what is coming next.

Why papers get rejected, or not, by journals

In theory, anything that contributes to the increase of world knowledge is worth publishing and reading. There are two limitations to this statement.

First, how substantial should the contribution be to the global knowledge of human species to deserve publishing? In a Hobbesian perspective, a picture of a cat contributes to world knowledge inasmuch as you have never seen that very cat in that very position before. Therefore, in such case, your knowledge, along with the ones who have never seen that cat in that position, will surely be enriched by that picture.

---

[2] Permission to reproduce the image was not received by the time this book had to be printed but you can check it at http://phdcomics.com/comics/archive.php?comicid=1121

Social media are providing an excellent setting to publish pictures of cats in any positions so let us move to the second limitation. Virtually anything, it may be argued, deserves publication. The question is by whom. It is not a matter of public ability but of niche and market segmentation. Depending on how much, and how, you advance knowledge, you may claim the right to be published in this or that outlet.

Academic journals, like any other outlets, have their own criteria, and their standards, that exclude most of the written production of this world. They publish long pieces of writing, based on some sort of scientific evidence, logic or reasoning, that allow world knowledge to advance based on facts analyzed through a scientific lens. But the change of the academic industry has forced some sort of standardization of scientific knowledge. If, some years ago, a nice digressive discourse, in a free form, had been acceptable by a prestigious journal, the English-speaking world would have moved towards a model that is more and more strict. There are exceptions, of course, and I would include pieces of knowledge produced by academic superstars. Some people are in such high demand, academically speaking but also for policy advice or essays, that they can allow themselves to publish in virtually any format.

For the rest of us, the starting model is clear. Once you master it, you can move away from it and add your own twist to the scheme. To start with, however, it might be worth sticking to:

- Introduction
- Literature
- Empirical evidence (and methodology for data collection and processing)
- Conclusion

As in the case of the perfect abstracts, it sounds thrillingly simple and all you need to do is to insert all the required elements in good shape. Then your paper becomes publishable by an academic journal. The kind of journal and its ranking will depend on the quality of your evidence and discussion, as well as many other factors, but your paper will at least be considered a paper worth consideration by a decent journal.

Introduction: most journals will expect to receive argumentative papers, so you will have to explain what the argument of your paper is. The argument may also be regarded as the main contribution to the paper. As one of my mentors once told me, the argument of the paper is like a jingle and you should ask yourself, "When people remember your paper, what is the jingle (1–2 lines) that you want them to sing in their head?" This is as much as people should remember of your paper. The rest is just demonstration and locating in debates. The paper will imply that so far, we know that much and that, in addition to what we know, a novel relationship should be considered. This could be a new theoretical paradigm, a challenge to an existing paradigm or simply something anomalous that current theories cannot explain). There are two consequences of the above.

The first is that, to be able to explain what the paper adds to debates and theories, you have to mention these theories and where they have stopped. Then, you can elaborate on it in the next section. But you have to do it and illustrate in which disciplinary, or interdisciplinary, debates your paper pinpoints it.

The second is that, if there are no debates that could serve as a basis. Your paper could be simply descriptive and not argumentative. But this is a slippery territory and often highly subjective. If the reviewers, or the editor of a journal, feel that your material is novel and innovative then you might be able to get away with little framing in relevant debates. In some other cases, more conservative or stricter reviewers will still demand what debates you engage with.

Existing debates or studies: to be able to explain the innovative nature of your paper, you need to illustrate on which existing studies and hypotheses you have based your data collection and processing. Where similar studies have arrived so far, what similar experiments or studies have shown or argued and what are the questions that have remained unanswered up until now. This is in case you want to give continuity to some streams of research. Alternatively, what are the assumptions that your paper is going to question, or challenge, and on what assumptions, or hypotheses, have you based your data collection and have constructed your paper.

Empirical evidence: this varies a lot across disciplines but in general it is the easier part to explain. Take your data, explain how you have processed them, and to which results they have led you. If the methodology is complex, you might need to provide more information about your methodological approach, its assumptions and its limitations. In papers where the methodology is simpler, a brief explanation of the approach can just be added to the introduction, with no separate section in the paper.

Conclusion: in my writing workshops, I often ask my participants whether they know the difference between a detective book and an academic paper. In a detective book, you make sense of the book (and learn who the murderer is) only in the last pages. In an academic paper, you need to make sense of the work (and realize that there is no murderer) in the first lines of the introduction.

I have noticed that a fraction of the academic community I am in touch with tends to interpret the conclusion of their paper as if they were writing a detective paper and hide the results and findings until the very last section. There is no need to do this. Your conclusion section should be a sort of decompression chamber. After an extensive explanation and engagement with your research, you need to bring a reader out while leaving them with a good sense of the paper. You should thus guide them and remind them what debates you have engaged in, what are their main shortfalls and what the paper has tried to show.

This sounds simple, but I find it extremely difficult, especially after the titanic effort that is required to edit an academic paper, rewriting it several times and putting most of your efforts so that the introduction and the other sections are well synchronized. As a result, I get to the conclusion completely drained and unmotivated. But bad conclusions can somehow spoil a paper so, in the end, you need to find the way to devote some attention and effort to it.

The wicked art of framing your research

My approach to reviewing other people's articles is that there is no bad paper. There are just papers that are not "baked" enough. In other words, some papers require just a little bit more extra work to become publishable. Some others require months, or perhaps a lifetime. But they have all the potential of becoming decent papers. How to reach quality is a matter of training, but not necessarily of strategy. This is why I leave the topic to those colleagues who work and can tell much more than I do on academic or creative writing. But, inasmuch as a low-quality paper at a given time is a major reason for rejection, the other one is that it is submitted to the wrong journal.

Submitting to the wrong journal is not just a matter of sending your paper on funeral practices to a journal of astrophysics. This may also happen, but it is easier to address than the incapacity of someone to understand the subtle, and sometimes invisible, differences between journals.

Critical studies vs mainstream: on the ideological positioning of a journal. Editorial boards of journals are made of people and these people, if they manage to work together, are alike to some fair extent. The sum of the ideological preferences of the editorial board can be defined as the journal's theoretical (and often ideological) position. People tend to fancy different theories, prefer some paradigms to others and be very critical of some others.

There are two extreme positions that I usually call "mainstream" and "critical" but could be named otherwise. What is important here is that some journals are close to what is more popular in a given field at a given time and some other journals prefer a more critical position. All journals, however, can be placed on a spectrum ranging from the "critical" to the "mainstream" position. Some will be more neutral, some others will embrace one or the other position, but they can all be located on a continuous line between these two. Likewise, some journals, even if officially multidisciplinary, will give preferences to certain approaches over others.

The more you submit a paper that is critical of the position a journal embraces, the more likely you are to get rejected. There will always be an exception and some genius colleague who makes it into the "wrong journal" by sending a splendid paper that the journal might respect and admire. But going into a Marxist journal with a mainstream position on IR is not necessarily a good idea. You can learn about the journal's position by word of mouth from other colleagues, or simply screening previously published papers. The reputation of journals in academia is relatively easy to learn about. There is always a colleague who has published in the journal you want to target, or that has been rejected. All the rest missing, you can always check online blogs on academic journals or the publications of the editorial board of that journal. This will give you an idea of what they prefer in terms of disciplines, approach, theory and ideology.

Empirical journals vs theoretical journals: even if, as I have mentioned elsewhere, a journal article should have a theoretical part and contribute to the construction, or deconstruction, of scientific paradigms, journals have a very different position on the proportion between empirics and theory that should be contained in a paper. Some friends submitted an article with good empirics to a major journal in their field. The journal liked the article and they went through the usual review process. By the time the article was ready to be published, 80% of the empirics had been taken out and the article had become extremely theoretical. Some empirics were left in, but their function was just to imply "We are basing our argument on facts that we collected and analyzed systematically, not on reflections under a tree." The main innovative part of the article was the theory. By contrast, some journals are happy with you elaborating the data you use, perhaps spend a bit more on methodology, and minimize the theoretical significance of your findings. Sending a mostly empirical article to a theoretical journal, and vice versa, increases the chances of rejection. Also, in this case, your homework can be done just by asking your colleagues, checking blogs but also reading the articles (or at least abstracts) of a few articles already published by that journal.

Country or area studies vs disciplinary studies: to conquer and maintain an audience, a journal must find its niche. There are journals that can allow themselves to publish almost anything, think of Nature or Science. But most of the journals have a certain readership that expects to find articles more or less consistent with their interests. They can focus on a topic, a discipline, a sub-discipline, or cover a given geographical area. The bigger (and more important) the journal is the wider its range of interests are. Sociology may have an ideological inclination but publishes sociological studies; the Journal of Biology publishes on a variety of biology-related topics. Some other journals occupy a very narrow niche and sound very specialized (e.g., Catalysis Survey from Asia).

If your research has produced empirical data, the methodology used to collect and process this data determines broadly the discipline(s) you are moving through. But which journal you target depends on how, and in which debates, you frame your data and what theoretical framework you construct.

Your research is at the center of your professional life but not everyone, and not every journal, will have the same attitude to it. Some will welcome what you do as it overlaps, partly or fully, with their research interests. Others will be not interested at all. Some others might become interested if you find a way to talk to them. As a good friend and colleague said, "The value of an article is its capacity to talk to audiences other than the ones it targets primarily."

In a disciplinary perspective, you should be able to go beyond your circle and compare your work to cognate studies with some elements in common or works focusing on other regions. You could try to use proxies, compare samples or populations but you should try to dialogue with other works. In an area-study perspective, you might want to explain how your findings refer to other findings from other countries from the same region and this is what is sometimes missing in an article. Indeed, I have seen many papers implying, "This article is so important because it is about the country I am studying and that is the center of my universe, so now it will be the center of your universe too." It is good to be passionate about a country, or a topic, but to contribute to a (global, disciplinary) debate you need to interest people beyond your narrow focus.

Thomas Eriksen is widely known for his works on Identity. His fieldwork has mostly been about Mauritius, a small island with a few million inhabitants. Still, when you work on identity, anywhere in the world, you need to take his works into account. Benedict Anderson's highly cited book "Imagined Communities" is one of the most important books on nationalism to date and scholars mostly remember his jingle "nations are made of imagined communities." But in his introduction, Anderson explains that his results, and conclusions, are based on evidence drawn in a particular world region. What region is so important? Both Anderson and Eriksen start from a narrow regional focus and address issues that are crucial to social theory. Their work, based on a very specific world region, end up talking to large portions of the academic community, to scholars working in anthropology, politics, history, sociology, regional studies and more.

The capacity of a paper to stick out of the mass lies not in its claim to address fundamental or world issues but in the authors' abilities to take a very small and narrow piece of knowledge and engage in a larger debate. It is an exercise leading to a dialogue across regions, disciplines, approaches: my approach complements existing ones in that that I propose something new, and relatively underexplored, in a region, discipline, area. The ultimate risk an author runs is that a paper only dialogues with itself, which can be called academic madness (think of someone talking to themselves on the street).

There is no unique, or single, way to "engage in a wider debate" since there is not one, but many debates you can connect to and the final decision may be the result of a complex choice. First, what debates do you want to contribute to? Where do you feel stronger and more prepared to bring some sort of contribution? Second, which journal you are submitting to.

How the same data evidence can be adapted to different contexts to approach different journals.
And why it will be rejected if you go to the wrong journal

NB: I am a social scientist and I mostly work on former USSR affairs so let me elaborate on what I know best keeping in mind that this is just an approach and that, changing names and disciplines, it can be replicated for other contexts, situations and disciplines.

Some time ago, my managing editor wrote to me because the author of a recently-submitted paper had sent an email asking for a fast peer-review process since the results presented in the paper, he claimed, were revolutionary.

Revolutionary for whom? And why, if ever, to my journal? I gave the author the benefit of doubt and sped up the process, after which the paper got rejected. Why?

What I saw in the process was an author who had conducted (possibly for the first time in his life) an empirical study of his own (small) country and was enthusiast about sharing it. He was so enthusiast about the topic, the research, the subject, he was sure that everyone else would love his work as much as he did. But things do not always work that way.

Let us assume that the paper presented novel, and original, data on poverty reduction in Georgia. I am taking Georgia since it is a small country and scholars would not consider it for a case study unless they have an interest in the region. In general, if you write about something marginal, you might have to work a bit more to intrigue your potential readership and eventually get read.

Let us also assume that the methodology used was sound and made sense, which is not always the case, and that the results had some kind of relevance for the country. The problem, in this and other cases, is not whether you have data but how you present them and how you contextualize them already from the beginning of the paper. Let us compare these four opening statements:

1. A large number of authors have maintained a positive correlation between X (e.g., poverty) and Y. However, a recent stream of empirically-based research has questioned this relationship because...using evidence from Georgia, this paper is intended to provide further evidence in this direction (or, alternatively, confirms the positive correlation between X and Y).

2. In post-socialist spaces, the relationship between X (poverty) and Y has been examined from a number of perspectives. A majority of scholars has found that...This paper gives continuity (or criticizes) these conclusions using the case of Georgia, in which we demonstrate that...

3. Since independence, Georgia has been adopting a number of measures to curb poverty. From measure X to measure Y, a number of interventions have led to different of results. This paper explores what interventions have been successful, or not, and why.

4. This paper presents the results of a survey on poverty reduction in Georgia. We find that measures are more likely to be successful under certain conditions (mention them) rather than others (mention them).

To me all four of the opening statements are acceptable. The question is where and by whom. Opening 3 and 4 are more empirical. They are more concerned about an assessment of data within a narrow national context and leave little room for comparison or to liaise with other studies. The article is likely to be appreciated by scholars from Georgian and Caucasus studies (if they want to do something similar in a neighboring country) or if someone is attempting a worldwide literature review on the topic. If I receive such a paper as a reviewer, my attitude will depend on the journal that has asked me to do the review.

With an opening statement like 3 or 4, the paper fits perfectly in a national journal (publishing studies on Georgia) and to some extent a regional one publishing studies on the Caucasus region. It might fit to some extent in a regional journal focusing on post-socialism or the post-Soviet region but, as a reviewer, I would at least ask the author to explain why someone studying, say, Kazakhstan, should be interested in the article's material and how the study could compare to similar studies conducted in the region. By contrast, an article starting with statement 2 would fit the scope of an area or regional journal well. Openings 2, 3 and 4 will not, however, be a good fit in any disciplinary journal, that are interested more in what these data (and their interpretations) mean for the advancement of the discipline than the data in themselves. For these journals, an opening statement like the first one is a much better match and should be followed by an analytical section engaging in debates beyond the country, and the region.

The table below summarizes possible attitudes, or reactions, of different journals to the opening statements mentioned above.

Journal/ statement	1	2	3	4
Journal of Georgian Studies	Nice, but can you expand the Georgia part?	Good to do a comparison but start from Georgian debates	Good match: we are interested in Georgia and your paper "explains Georgia"	Good match: we are interested in Georgia and your paper "explains Georgia"
Journal of Caucasus Studies	Nice but please reduce theory and explain more about the region and the context	Nice but please reduce theory and explain more about the region and the context	Interesting and relevant. If possible, mention some parallel studies in other Caucasus countries	Interesting and relevant. If possible, mention some parallel studies in other Caucasus countries

Journal of Post-USSR Studies	Well framed, but perhaps you might want to go for a theoretical journal?	Good match	Interesting perspective but it might be worth expanding the regional dimension	Interesting perspective but it might be worth expanding the regional dimension
Journal of European Development	Well framed, we can take it for review	Good post-Soviet perspective but Europe is larger than that, can you please compare perhaps with EU countries?	Georgia is interesting inasmuch as it allows us to better understand development from a European perspective, please add	How do your findings on Georgia confirm, or challenge, findings from other European regions?
Journal of World Development	Well framed, we can take it for review	The paper's scope is limited. Please expand to consider global development theories	Georgia is interesting inasmuch as it allows us to better understand development from a global perspective, please add	How do your findings on Georgia confirm, or challenge, findings from other world regions or general development theory?
Journal of Critical Development	Well framed, we can take it for review	The paper's scope is limited. Please expand to consider critical development theories	Georgia is interesting inasmuch as it allows us to criticize some major theories, please add	How do your findings on Georgia relate to mainstream theory and allow them to question it?

Methodological choices, and dilemmas

It is not possible to exhaust the totality of the possible methodological approaches that you could use for a paper, and there are much better manuals explaining to you how to develop your own methodology. If I mention methodology here, my concerns are two.

First, that your methodological choices should inform your strategic choice of the outlet you target for your paper. For one thing, going with a regression in a journal of anthropology is not an option. Even if the topic fits the journal and the theories you want to use are well known to the journal's readers, chances are that reviewers will not understand your methodology, will not appreciate it, or both. Therefore, before choosing a target journal, check what is the range of methodological approaches that they have published in the past. Also check what are the main methodological paradigms that the editorial board, and thus the journal, tend to prefer.

Second, the methodology is one of the easiest things to criticize in an article. You need not convince the reviewer that your choices are correct, as there will always be someone who disagrees with your methodological choices. You need, rather, to share the reasoning that led you to combine the methods in a way that the reviewer understands your logic and, even if they disagree, can agree that scientifically the sequence of methods, combined the way you did, makes some sense.

Besides, there is always the question of how much detail should you go into to explain your methodology. Some reviewers, and journals, care more than others. Some methodologies are extremely innovative whereas some others simply consist of applying something already well known, and established, to a different population, or sample. If your paper features a novel, and or experimental, methodological approach then it might be worth to spend a few hundred words to explain it. Your methodology, in this case, will be part of the contribution of your paper to scientific knowledge in the journal's field. By contrast, if you are just applying a simple regression, you could briefly explain the variables and the hypotheses used to choose these variables and then use the rest of the space in the paper to concentrate on what is really innovative in it.

How much is too much? On overpopulated bibliographies

Think about publishing, or just writing, in the pre-Internet era. Your knowledge would have to come from books, you would have to physically go to the library. Depending on where you are based, your library might have many or few books (or none), or journals, on the topic you want to write about. But how would you know, amongst the books available, which one is best for you, or has the best reputation, especially if you are at the beginning of your career?

I would imagine the most effective way would be to talk to someone who suggests you one, or several books. You would then have to find out which library has them and go through intra-library loans, travel to places, find illegal photocopies somewhere, or at least notes based on that book, to get acquainted with some parts of it. In such conditions, writing a literature review would be a titanic effort and you would sweat every single book you cite.

Think of a literature review in the Internet era. You choose a topic, type a keyword in a search engine and the page explodes with results, all nicely related to what you want to write about. Before the Internet it was hard to populate a bibliography, nowadays it is almost impossible not to over-populate it. This means that your new task is not to be able to get that very book and to read it but to make a choice among the thousands of books available. You first have to identify as many books and articles as possible but also, and more importantly, to quickly understand and select which ones are crucial for you and your research, for two reasons. One is that you have no material time to read all the literature that has been proposed to you by your search engine. The other is that, even if you manage to read everything, you have no sufficient space in your bibliography, to cite everything. A bibliography, on average, should occupy no more than 10–15% of the total amount of words in an article. However, in my view, this really depends on the context. An empirical experimental paper can look fine with a very short bibliography, whereas a literature review article should incorporate as many articles as possible.

With limited space, you should avoid citing works that bring little or nothing to your argument. A way to proceed could be by ranking publications on the same topic and choose only the ones at the top of your list. In a pro-establishment fashion, one could consider that, the more a work is cited, the more it is vital to cite it. However, this is also the conclusion one could reach after thinking pragmatically. The most cited works in your field are also likely to be the most famous ones (although not necessarily the most important ones). If your reviewer is an expert, they are likely to know them, and notice their absence, more than those that are less visible, and famous. By contrast, if your reviewer is not an expert in your narrow field and wants to do a check of your literature, they are likely to find most cited works before less cited ones.

That said, it is up to you to find the balance between what you think might be expected from you and what you feel is important for your article, to defend your choices, and to explain why a particular work was included, or not, in your paper. As a general rule, if a paper on a related topic has 10.000 citations it makes sense strategically to add it to your bibliography even if you do not like it or do not agree with its results. You may criticize it in your paper, but you are likely to be asked by the reviewers why you did not cite it, in case.

The wicked "I" in an article

The number of articles, and works, written in the first person has significantly increased in the past years. I like to place the origin of this phenomenon in the social sciences revolution started by Clifford Geertz in the 1960s, but it is in the past ten or so years that I have witnessed a sharp increase of articles written in first person. The problem, that sometimes can reach unexpected proportions, is the use of "I" in a single-authored paper. Used moderately, in some disciplines and contexts, the narrating "I" can make the reading pleasant and more fluid. The problem is that moderation is not always applied, and you can end up reading an article where the "I" is used every second sentence, a thing that is likely to give you goosebumps or you simply get tired of the paper after the first page.

Think of being a reviewer of that paper. You read it and find "I" used 200–250 times throughout the text. It basically brings the attention back to the researcher, instead of having them as the median and a lens to look through the material collected. It reads ego-centric to the point that the main topic of the paper is not the research but the researcher. It also raises a question about the positionality of an author and why they need to be so present during data collection.

I have read some very nice works written in a narrating "I." I remember a PhD thesis about unfaithful relationships of football players during the NFL season. The thesis was written by the wife of one of the football players using self-ethnography and she had little choice other than to use "I," but this choice comes with a risk. You get tired while writing, you get too passionate about your topic, you want to share too much and the wicked "I" pops up throughout your article, like mushrooms after it rains.

Instead of "I" you might want to use "we," it might sound old-fashioned, but it might be a way to contain your ego, which otherwise tends to impose itself if you use "I." This could solve some of your problems since the team speaks out and guides the reader through the paper. Besides, in a multi-authored paper it is likely that several authors will read the text before sending it and, if "we" is used too much throughout the paper, some of the authors will notice it and reduce its use, a thing that will not happen on a single-authored paper.

There is no formal rule on when to use or not use "I" but, if you use it, try to alternate it with other forms such as the passive form (it will be shown; it will be suggested) or use "this article" (this study, this research) as subject of the sentence. My advice would be, if you decide to use "I" try to construct every sentence without it and use "I" only when it is impossible, too complicated, or confusing not to use it. If you cannot avoid it or think the article would read much more solid when narrated by you, then go for it. But then do a final check of how many times you have used "I" throughout the article before submitting it.

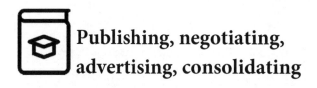

Publishing, negotiating, advertising, consolidating

How to get in a good publication?

What a "good publication" is and that "good" means is very subjective, depending on whom you want to please. That said, ending up publishing an article, or a book, with the journal or press you were targeting depends on a number of circumstances.

First is, obviously, that you write something and that "that something" makes sense. But where, how and (most importantly) by whom this is published mostly rests on you having invested time in getting to know the right people or, at least, happening to be in the right place at the right time. If the editor of a top journal was someone you have studied with, or is your best friend, you definitely have higher chances to get published there than an unknown fellow.

This is why conferences are important. It is not only about listening to presentations but to meet and mingle with the maximum possible amount of people. I remember conferences where I spent 90% of my time at book exhibitions. Most people would be attending panels but, at the exhibition, I would find people who were likeminded or who were in the same mood as I was (no listening, just rumbling around). In the end, there is always someone there who is skipping a session and it is at the book exhibitions that you can meet publishers or even get a book contract. It is very subjective, but I definitely prefer to stay in public areas than in session rooms at most large conferences.

> ### Case study: right places, right time, right topic—Cambridge University Press
>
> Some years ago, a friend organized a seminar on fieldwork in non-Western environments. There I met someone who, at the time was about to submit his PhD on warlords in Afghanistan. Definitely a sexy topic in many respects. Not surprisingly he received an offer from Cambridge University Press. Here is how it went, according to what he told me.

> He was at the conference and noticed the Cambridge University Press booth. He told a friend that he would need, at some point, to find a publisher for his PhD thesis. His friend replied, "Just go and ask." He went over, asked what to do to publish with them.
>
> He was asked in which university he was enrolled and the topic of his research. His university was excellent and known for producing excellent PhD theses. The topic was catchy and very in fashion at the time. He was also lucky enough to speak directly with the commissioning editor, who immediately gave him an oral agreement to publish with them. We can assume that he had to work a lot to deliver the manuscript that, most likely, got grilled by the reviewers. Nonetheless, by being at that conference and happening to talk to the editor he bypassed many steps that most of us would have to undergo.
>
> Another colleague got a contract with Cambridge through another coincidence. Representatives of the publishers went to deliver an information session at the university where he was on a post-doctoral fellowship and invited all attendants to submit their manuscripts. As much as this may sound odd—Cambridge soliciting manuscripts—it is also logical. Cambridge University Press lives by publishing books. To publish them they need to find authors and by recruiting authors when they are not famous, but promising, is an excellent strategy. By going to a top university and gathering recipients of a prestigious fellowship they maximize their chances to receive high-quality submissions. The process, if I am not wrong, took him 5 years but with a monograph published by Cambridge University Press he is now in some sort of "Olympus" of scholars.

Many people try for ages to get a contract with Cambridge University Press, often with no success, and these colleagues got it through an apparently painless process. I am sure this is the short version of the story and they had to work a lot still, but it is emblematic of how academia works. Sometimes you get published not necessarily because your paper is the best one (even if both colleagues are smart and excellent writers, I have no doubts about their quality of work), but simply because you are in the right place at the right time.

The situations above show how hard and easy it is, at the same time, to land a good publisher. But there is an important step before that. The best papers, or books, are not the ones that are still to be written but the ones that have already been written. I hear many colleagues huffing "that scholar is not very original," or "I do not like the quality of that person's work," or even "My work is much better, but nobody seems to notice." It serves no purpose to criticize someone else's work thinking (in order to claim) that your work is better. As long as this person has produced a paper and you have not he is winning 1-0 just because he has something written and you do not.

Once you write, even before publishing, you have a lot of marketing ahead to do. How otherwise would people notice you in the sea of academic works that are produced every year in your area or in your field? It is not just "I write a paper and then I wait, and then somebody reads it and says 'wow,' that's the best paper in the world!" You will probably have to work with someone and exchange ideas. You might have to convince fellow academics, amongst whom are possibly a few established scholars, that your work is worth reading. I often think of the situation when you hear a song on the radio and think that it is not that special. Then, after listening to it several times you start liking and, in the end, it becomes one of your favorite songs for a certain period. I do not think the way academic marketing works is so different. You can start with a "not bad" or even "anonymous" paper and end up thinking "that is actually very interesting."

We are humans, emotions evolve, change and are circumstantial. You did not think something was relevant to you or to your work and then you change your topic and then someone's work becomes relevant to what you do. Or your perspective changes and you realize that a given work, that you ignored before, is actually worth reading. Or else, you do not notice an author until you meet them at a conference and end up drinking a coffee (or having a few too many beers) with them. Then you feel it is your moral obligation to at least know what the person is doing, and you end up liking not only the person but their work.

By the same token, quality alone will not bring you far. You may be the best author ever, but nobody will know it until they read you. And because there are thousands of more papers competing with yours, you need to induce people to read you. A good way is to be promoted, and supported, by some senior scholars who think that your intellectual capacity is very strong. If you get open support by someone more established, for instance by working with them, you will immediately become more visible. In such case, you are not only "yourself." You become the one working with Prof X. Of course, at some stage, you need to detach yourself from Prof X if you want to develop some autonomy. But you may also choose not to and build a career praising yourself as Prof X favorite's disciple. Whatever strategy you choose, the message here is that you need to unpack your attitudes with regards to many aspects of academic life to be able to develop your career.

Officially we do research, we write and teach and a few of us want, and choose, to enter academic politics. But we often forget other aspects: marketing, advertising, networking, develop alliances, cultivate enemies, debate, go public and, above all, we sometimes forget the most important one—to enjoy what we do. This can only happen if we understand the range of qualities and actions required from us, rank them and give priority to some in order to find a balance between the things that we are expected to do and the few that we really like to do. If we lose this focus, why stay in academia?

How to get your article accepted? (some strategic considerations on the peer review process)

In an ideal world, an article is accepted by a journal depending on its quality. Good: in; bad: out. However, we are not in an ideal world and the boundary between a good and a bad article is never so clear-cut. I would rephrase it this way: an article gets accepted if the reviewers and the editor in chief like it or think it is worth publishing. It is not in the opposite case.

This means that, inasmuch as the peer review process can be regarded as objective—any peer-reviewed journal would have two or more peers who look at your work and provide a report along with the guidelines of that journal, judgment and assessment of an article is subjective and changes across disciplines, regions, people and personalities. This tends to affect the publication process and eventually results into articles of very different quality being published in the same journal.

Let us look at the anatomy of a peer review.

From an editor's perspective, once I receive an article, I have two options: I read the article or pass it immediately to the reviewers. This depends on the journal policy but also on my personal choice and, ultimately, on the number of submissions per month that I receive.

Sending an article for an external review is a "cost," meaning that once you ask someone to review an article you cannot ask the same person to review another article for you for some time. You will need to invest time and resources into searching for further reviewers if you receive additional papers on that particular subject. Besides, if a reviewer receives a low-quality article from a journal, they might form a lower opinion of that journal. As a result, you might thus want, as editor in chief, to initially invest some time to screen the articles and reject the ones where the quality is below a certain standard to diminish the number of reviewers you need to rely on at a given stage.

From an author's perspective, I see three ideal types of reviewers: the nice ones, the frustrated ones and those that the editor does not know. Of these three categories, you have those who write a review quickly and those who are slow. Advantages and disadvantages of each of the reviewers are illustrated in the matrix below.

	Fast	Slow
Nice	Constructive review, sometimes hard but full of good ideas and delivered quickly (my ideal reviewer)	Constructive review but worth waiting (my second-best reviewer)
Frustrated	Destructive review, often in competition with your paper or ideas—e.g., like "I know this better, why are you studying this?"—I do not understand it (to-avoid reviewer)	Equally destructive but you might have to wait months before getting them back (to-avoid-even-more reviewer)
Unknown	Anything could happen, but you get a response fast	Anything could happen, but you also have to wait

As an author, you want all reviewers to be nice and fast. How to increase your chances of getting the ideal reviewer, or at least someone who will criticize you constructively?

1. Submit to the right journal: if the journal covers your article's topic, it is more likely that the editor in chief has a personal network of reviewers who are more familiar with your topic and knows personally a number of people who could review your article.

2. Interest the journal: if the editor likes the topic of your article, they will be interested in giving it to reviewers who are nicer. Sometimes they might even warn them "I am interested in this article, please do not destroy it too much."

3. Know the editor in chief, when possible. Ideally, you have met them at a conference and spent some time together, but that is not always the case. However, even a short email warning them that your proposal will come might "prepare" the editor and create some sympathy towards your article.

You can meet these three conditions relatively easily, but they are almost automatic when you submit an abstract, that is then accepted, for a special issue (see question below on special issues). In that case, the guest editors will declare their interest in your topic. They will also have an interest in publishing it because it will be among the ones needed to fill the special issue. As a result, they might review your article themselves with a sympathetic eye or give it to someone warning them "It's for a special issue, please do not be too hard or the special issue will simply not happen."

Depending on the extent to which you meet the conditions above, the quality of your article and the opinion of the reviewers, you may end up with a wide range of outcomes.

What are the possible outcomes of a peer review process and what is their hidden message?

As a reviewer, you can suggest the following options for an article.

Accept. This means that a reviewer is entirely satisfied with your work. I have hardly ever seen, or experienced, unconditional acceptance but it may happen. However, it is a difficult decision to make and it will expose you. If anyone finds a flaw in the article, then you are indirectly under accusation for not having checked the article properly or having missed something. This is why a review suggesting unconditional acceptance of an article usually comes either from a very established academic who is confident enough to say, "this is good" or by someone who does not really care about the article. Anyone else wishing to stay on the safe side will suggest at least minor revisions.

Minor revisions required. The reviewer is mostly satisfied with the article but points out some minor things needed to improve it. Minor revisions might be a few typos but also some small parts to rewrite. There is no agreed standard and minor revisions might even mean changing a whole section. However, it is a clear message that publication is recommended.

Major revisions required. With this, the reviewer enters an ambiguous territory. It means that the paper is not publishable as it is. It could be a softer way (than open rejection) to communicate that the paper is not ready but substantial work is needed. It could also be a way to say, "The paper is already decent, but I want my recommendations to be taken seriously into account." I once received two reviews suggesting "major revisions" and a letter of rejection. My interpretation is that the journal had a high turnover of articles, and therefore already a high number of works accepted with minor revisions. As a result, the editor thought that bringing my article to publication was not worth the effort. Or the editor simply did not like us. That also happens.

One mistake you might not want to make when receiving a request for major revisions is to resubmit it 2 weeks after receiving the comments. Comments, especially if substantial, need to be "digested" before being transformed into amendments and, as an editor, I look at papers that are immediately resubmitted with suspicion. How could such major amendments, requiring time and reflections, be completed in such a short time?

Once an editor receives a paper resubmitted after major revisions have been suggested, they might want to ensure that all of the main issues have been addressed. Even if not required, you might invest your time and write a letter explaining how the comments have been addressed (or ignored, explaining why you deemed them not relevant). That will show that you have taken the journal's opinion seriously into account. Alternatively, you can also highlight the changes in the body of the new article. At any rate, and as a general rule, guiding the reader is always a good idea.

Reject and resubmit (or revise and resubmit). This case is not far from major revisions, at least for me, even if it sounds much worse. I see this as the reviewer suggesting that some substantial amount of time, and efforts, are needed and in no way the authors should consider resubmitting something before having gone through the paper a few times and introducing a significant number of changes and amendments.

Reject (definitive and final). Once I received feedback for an article submitted to my journal, "This paper should not be published in the current or any other forms." I found this attitude arrogant. How can you foresee to what extent the author will be able to grow intellectually and state that they will be never able to amend a paper? For me, a paper is measured against time, not quality. My question is, "How many more days, months, or years of work are needed to make this paper publishable?" If the answer is six months or more, then I reject it. Some papers are just born very early, need further reasoning, while some others need further reading. In some more extreme cases, the authors might need full (re)training or further development of some skills. A paper with a terrible methodological approach might mean that the authors need some months, or years, of further methodological training. Therefore, I reject the paper to give them the time to undergo that training but with no claims that they will never reach a level allowing publication.

Why not to publish in a special (guest-edited) issue of a journal?

I once invited an American colleague to write an article for a special issue of a journal that I was co-editing with a friend. His answer, between awkward and frightened, was that he thought he should prioritize standard issues because, according to the evaluation criteria he was aware of, an article in a special issue counted less, towards tenure, than one in a standard issue. In other words, at least theoretically, it would be better for him to publish in the same journal (that was a very good one) but without me as a guest editor.

I was shocked. This made little sense to me strategically. Given the position of the journal, that special issue would have been read by anyone with an interest in the target region and he would then be considered the expert on whatever topic he proposed. He would be, in other words, part of an elite team of scientists working on a given topic, and region, from a variety of perspectives. He would also have the chance to work alongside with people with similar interests, expanding his contacts and eventually widening the scope of his collaborations.

This is not to say that I do not empathize with him. I understood the pressure he was under as a tenure-track professor and the fact that he had to devote any and every effort to getting tenure, after which he would probably become freer to publish wherever he wanted. But his logic was a very short-term one, as often happens in life, seeing only the immediate effect of his action but failing to understand the long-term consequences. A publication with us would have probably brought him many more benefits, opening numerous doors leading to more publications and definitely giving him more visibility. This is the same logic I apply when I am asked to write a book chapter, which brings me virtually no formal benefits. I base my decision on whether I see possible alternative benefits that the book chapter will bring me in the medium or long run (see section on why to write a book chapter).

The above distinction does not exist, at least at present, in most systems where few will bother checking if the article is part of a special issue or not. But I have to admit that I understand the logic. Publishing in a special issue is allegedly easier, provided that the guest editors are fairly decent managers (otherwise it turns into a nightmare).

Why to publish in a special (guest-edited) issue of a journal?

A special, or guest, issue of a journal is an issue, or a double issue, edited by one or more guest editors on a specific theme agreed between the editors and the editorial board of the journal. It might be in addition to the usual number of issues published per year or it might just be within it, but under the guidance of people other than the usual editor(s). Depending on the journal's policy, one or more tasks may be handed out to the guest editor(s), from soliciting papers to the whole reviewing and copy-editing processes. There is no real agreed standard, but the general rule is that guest editors have sufficient margin to choose their authors, decide on the quality of the papers and have responsibility to submit on time a number of papers (including an editorial, see the section on "why to edit a special issue") that will fill the issue. It is likely that the usual editor will want to see the papers and have the last word on their quality. However, unless the editor is a control freak, their role will be confined to that and to general correspondence with the guest editors.

There are at least two advantages, from an author's perspective, in submitting to a special issue of a journal: lower risk of rejection and higher guidance throughout the submission process.

Lower rejection risk. A journal existing for many years can be regarded as a permanently ongoing process, with articles regularly coming in and being published at some point. In contrast, a special issue is a project with a beginning and an end. It cannot count on previously submitted papers and cannot publish papers that are submitted late.

A standard editor of a journal with a decent turnover could not care less if some paper is late or of low quality (unless they have a hole in an upcoming issue). If the journal is established already, they would have a regular flow of submissions (measured as X papers per month) and each issue is filled well in advance. Some authors will be late with their resubmission, and thus delayed to a later issue, some other authors will be faster and could fill in any issues with an insufficient number of papers.

A special issue is a different story and it entails a higher risk. It moves outside the usual channels the journal uses and possibly taps from a separate pool of authors, who are attracted to a particular journal thanks to a topic, or the chance to work with the guest editors. Guest editors have to face a strategic choice to populate a special issue: too many vs just enough.

Launching a call for abstracts gives you an indication of how much interest there is around the special issue you propose but, once abstracts are in, you need to accept some authors and reject the others. How many can you accept for, say, a special issue containing 8 papers? A good abstract does not always lead to a good paper and authors might be late, or not have enough time to deliver a good quality paper so in terms of risk management, accepting only 8 abstracts is a risk. One author is late, one delivers a bad paper and your special issue goes bananas. You can try the other way and accept 20 abstracts, confident that at least 8 of them will deliver a publishable piece of work. But what if then 15 of them deliver a good article and on time? Where would you put the extra 7 papers? You could negotiate with the journal to include one extra article in your special issue, but you would have to reject 5–6 authors simply by virtue of not having enough space and this would definitely not benefit your reputation or your professional relationship with the rejected authors.

How many abstracts to accept, and thus how many papers to solicit, is a personal choice. Only you know the perspective authors, how many of them are likely to deliver good quality work and what to do with the excluded ones. Whatever approach you choose the reality is that, compared to a standard issue managed by a standard editor in chief, you have more limited time, option and papers. As a result, each of the abstracts, and of the resulting papers, might be vital to your special issue and the cost of rejecting a paper might be high. You reject too many papers, or submit too few to the journal, and your special issue has to be canceled.

Higher guidance. In contrast with submission to a standard issue, where you just upload a paper into the system, there is some sort of pre-selection process when submitting to a special issue of a journal. Perspective authors will be requested to submit an abstract that, if selected, should then be turned into a paper. This requires additional work from you in the preparation phase (there is no need to send an abstract if you submit it to a standard issue) and there is no guarantee that your abstract will be selected. However, once your abstract is selected you are "almost in." First, acceptance of your abstract means that the editors are interested in your topic and will give full consideration to your paper. Second, for a guest editor of a special issue, the cost of rejecting a paper (whose abstract had been accepted) is higher than for an editor of the journal. Too many papers rejected means that the special issue might not see the time of day. Your loss will thus become also their loss, so much so that they might try to help you as much as possible, to get your piece published. I even remember a case when I submitted a paper that both reviewers suggested to reject, but the editors were still willing to give me a chance. I pulled out in the end, but that was indicative of the way the process had been handled. Indeed, how many standard journals would give such consideration to a rejected paper?

Case study—genesis of a journal publication (from the Scopus diaries blog)

Preparing an article for a special issue could be a way to get published faster...or a pain in the neck. What would be your strategy and attitude?

Another article is out; a good impact factor and a well-respected journal. This might be seen as a standard achievement mid-career scholar. We are paid to produce knowledge and get it validated by sending it to academic journals, that are considered of good quality, and where people (mostly scholars, if any) will allegedly read it and take advantage of our work.

But this is not a post to celebrate how good we were in banging this piece into a good journal. This is about the genesis of the article and how we got to publish it where it is now.

I had initially received an invitation to participate in a special issue by a colleague and friend into an area study journal.

To be honest, I stopped considering that very journal as a potential target—and this post will not improve the situation, I guess—after its editorial board had been changed and the journal renamed to the surprise, and shock, of some of its founders.

I had met the new editor at a conference and he seemed friendly and open-minded. we had some good chats and, once he became editor, I submitted a proposal for a special issue that was accepted. Shortly after, the special issue was pulled out because the editor basically rejected every single article that our authors submitted with no chance of appeal.

I was not enthusiast at the idea of dealing with the journal once again, but I decided that I was ready to run the risk for the sake of working with my colleague, who could eventually act as a buffer between us.

Not having much time to write (when do academics have enough time to write?) I involved two trusted colleagues of mine (who probably know much more about the topic than I do) and we submitted, first, an abstract and then a full paper to the journal.

After some months we received the responses from the reviewers. They were somehow neutral: pointed out some major issues of the article but neither reviewer suggested rejection.

Still, the article was rejected. I received a personal email from the editor in chief mentioning that, in the case the reviewers are undecided, the editor has the right to decide and he had decided to reject us.

I was upset but not surprised. Given my past experiences with the editor, I had taken into account that this could happen. In the end, we adjusted the article following the reviewers' comments and it went into another journal. I had done a review for them and I had loved the way the journal was managed. Briefly, I sent the article, got the reviews, reworked the article a few times with my colleagues and it was accepted.

Fast turnover, constructive criticism and easy-going editors. A painless process that I would recommend to everyone, in contrast with the previous one.

However, this story is not to moan against a journal or a person. Some attitudes are extremely common in academia. I decided to write this post because this experience is extremely valuable as a case study to share two considerations.

First: special issues

They are usually ways to get published fast and painlessly but there are exceptions. One is when the guest editors are not good managers and will kill you with micro tasks, delayed answers and make all of your worst nightmares come true.

The other is when the editor in chief wants to be in full control of everything. A special issue (edited by a guest editor) is based on trust and understanding. Understanding that there might be opinions that differ from yours (the ones of your guest editors or their authors), that there might be things that you (as editor in chief) understand less than your authors or guest editors. Trust that your guest editors will deliver a quality standard that is acceptable for your journal. Otherwise, why to hand out a special issue to someone?

On these premises we can identify two opposite positions by an editor in chief:

1) I give you a special issue but do not bother me with anything. I want a final, and finalized, product that I can send to production after a quick look.

2) I want full control on your special issue, will personally check every step you make and ensure that it is up to my standards.

Neither position is healthy, but these are ideal types. In reality most, not to say all, editors in chief will be in between these two when dealing with a special issue. Choose your own favorite option but be aware that either of the situations above might happen to you.

Second: the power of an editor in chief

Even if the peer review process has been conceived to ensure quality for published articles, and, even if the existence of editorial boards guarantees some democratic standards within a journal and diminishes the power of the editor in chief, the reality is one: editors have a tremendous amount of power and discretion when it comes to the acceptance/reject choice.

They can reject an article that the reviewers did not suggest rejecting (well, not directly) or save an article that the reviewers suggested to reject. They can, above all, select the reviewers and decide whether to hand the article over to someone who will destroy it or someone who will use a light touch.

This is unfair? Well, life is unfair, and I do not think we can change this. There will always be some editors in chief who like you and will be ready to look carefully at what you write and others who will prioritize other people.

Select your favorite editors in chief, befriend them and build alliances and networks based on whom you like or find pleasant to work with. I do not believe I am saying anything new but that's my advice for today.

How to get invited to deliver a guest lecture?

Passing a peer review or any other kind of barriers you might encounter will give you symbolic power (you are good enough to publish in a given journal) but still, people need to find out what you have done. The academic equivalent of word of mouth is a guest lecture. How to get invited? Well, you might simply invite yourself.

In my dreams, a guest lecture happens when, while working on my book in my studio, someone calls me through my secret line (the one used by Batman and other superheroes) to ask if I can come and deliver a talk at their university. This is not how it works, or how it has worked for me at least. I have received invitations to deliver guest lectures (not through my Bat-line, but by more banal e-mail). I could simply meet somebody at a conference and mention that am visiting somewhere near in the next months. Then they say, "Why don't you deliver a lecture in my department?" and the deal is on.

A guest lecture may happen in any university, or institution, other than yours. Of course, everyone dreams of a guest lecture at Harvard or Yale but a guest lecture in any other university is a way to meet people and get them to read your things they would not read otherwise. In this respect, consider even delivering seminars at your own university, where people from other departments, or other institutions from the same city, might come and get acquainted with your work and yourself.

The amount of people who will autonomously decide to read your work is, in principle, low but then go there, deliver a nice presentation and people start to think that you are someone worthy of attention. In academia, it is difficult to hit thousands of readers. We rather rely on smaller circles of people who are fond of your work. A guest lecture is a chance to make people associate your work with your face and your personality and eventually get a bit more visibility. It is also a chance to get feedback from other people, a thing that might even lead to new collaborations or further invitations elsewhere. The way to Harvard is still long but we all need to start somewhere.

Why should I organize a panel at a conference?

Sounds obvious but it is worth reflecting on. Conferences (or workshops) are excellent opportunities to make your work visible. However, this does not happen magically, at least not at the beginning of your career. Let us start with the worst possible strategy: submit an abstract to a random conference. In a best-case scenario, they put you into a panel with someone extremely famous and you will present in a room full of people, or even get to interact with your more established colleagues. If you play your chances well you might even interest them, interest the public, or both. But what are the odds of this happening? It is more likely that they will put you on an anonymous graveyard panel on the last day, when most people are already leaving or have left.

Conferences are for networking, but networking is well important before the conference. You might want to try and be placed into a panel with people who are more advanced than you in their academic career. In contrast to what one might be inclined to think, this is easier and happens with more frequency than one might expect. A star, to become and remain a star, needs supporters. They need administrative work and marketing, two things into which not everyone is willing to invest. If you, as a junior scholar, offer to do most of the dirty work for them and offer some fair and decent options, chances are that they will accept to work with you. Some years ago, I wanted to maximize the amount of people attending my book presentation at a major conference. I wrote to a colleague who is a star in the field and asked him whether he would be interested in delivering a joint book presentation. He simply had to come and speak about his book in the frame of our session. He agreed and saved hours of administrative work that I took upon myself. But I gained a large share of the public that came for his book and also listened to my presentation.

When you start your career, you might want to take most of the administrative burden related to articles, books, conference panels, on yourself. Once you get more established you lose some motivation, energy, time and you need people who can do this for you, or with you. At first, you look for co-editors, and co-organizers, who can take some of the more mechanical work or at least who can share tasks with you. Think when you want to go running or cycling in the evening. The legs are yours, the body is yours, but if you have someone to interact with you, you end up more motivated. The principle is the same when editing. You still have to use your head to do it but at least you can share a joke, a comment, and/or frustration with someone.

When I edited my first book, I did most of the administrative work myself. Now I look for co-editors who can help me with this. I am simply not motivated enough, or have not enough time, to complete all the tasks myself. The same happens when I organize a panel for a conference. I will have 1–2 people in mind but I am happy if someone (whose research interest are in line with the panel's logic) offers an abstract and is ready and responsive to participate in the panel. When I was serving as section chair for some major conferences, and in charge of filling 10–12 panels with around 60 presentations, I was glad when some of my colleagues came to me and asked to submit a whole panel. That was less work for me and would ensure that that panel in my section was consistent and of decent quality.

If you have someone in mind that you want to meet, then you can look them up in the program and go to their presentation. But you can also anticipate things and write to them. Chances are that they wanted to attend but did not have time to prepare a panel or simply to think of a paper. Knowing that someone is directly interested in their work might be an extra motivation for them. And in the end, you will end up drinking tea or a beer with someone you always wanted to meet but never had the chance to. I have been surprised by how many people I did not expect to meet (and whose existence I ignored) became good colleagues or even friends simply because I met them at a conference and we liked each other. In the end, if someone likes you as a person it is more likely that they will get interested in your work, cite you, propose collaborations in the future. This is why for me conferences are not just an excuse to present my work but a chance to meet people.

Should I use PowerPoint for my presentation?

I have to confess that I have reached very high levels of intolerance towards PowerPoint presentations. They may be extremely useful, especially if you have visual material to show. But a great majority of them seem to over-rely on it. PowerPoint is an audio-visual tool, that helps make your presentation better, by tidying and organizing things. It is not a magic stick that makes a boring presentation into an interesting one. Among the most common mistakes I classify the attempts to stuff hundreds of words onto a slide, use long quotations and, especially, use your PowerPoint presentations as your personal notes, the ones you should have in front of you to help you structure your presentation. The more that is included in the PowerPoint, the more the presenter merely reads from the slides and the less I understand why the presenter is there to speak. This attitude, taken to its limits, could simply encourage the organization of a session where each one is read in silence by the public, to then get discussed publicly.

In many respects, the use of PowerPoint is the perfect excuse not to work on your presentation and communication skills, letting your computer speak for you. In contrast, a thing that I like to remind the audience a lot of when I am presenting is that there was life before PowerPoint. It is, of course, a provocation because some presentations become much better with PowerPoint, but this is to challenge the "moral pressure" that when you present you need to have a PowerPoint presentation to show. You need it only if it adds value to what you want to say, if it helps people better understand your argument. PowerPoint is not a replacement but a complement. If you need a scheme for yourself then draw it on a piece of paper and follow it. If you read directly from your PowerPoint presentation, chances are that you will lose the audience's attention quickly.

Ideally, PowerPoint would be a way to make people visualize what you are talking about, but the main attention should still be on you. This will also give you the chance to work on your presentation skills, the tone of your voice, your body language, the speed at which you talk and the amount of information you want to convey.

I have seen people reading their presentation from their paper. I think this is one of the worst things you might do. First, it is very likely that you will not be able to stick to the time allocated to you; second you are busy reading and your voice will be boringly flat; third, there is no guarantee that you will be able to devote the amount of time needed to the points you wanted to emphasize. I understand this might be a way to deliver a presentation in a language you do not know well but you might as well put down some bullet points with the words you want to use. In the end, making things simple might be the best solution.

Many times, with colleagues or friends, we have been surprised by the way people fill PowerPoint slides with loads of words and try to fit in as much as possible. I believe the quality of a slide does not depend on the amount of information you put in but on how easy it is to understand it. Sometimes less is more, a few words are better than an overfilled slide. Next time you go to a conference try to deliver a presentation without PowerPoint, then think what you really missed while presenting. This is what should then go into your PowerPoint.

Why should I try and popularize science? (on targeting the general public)

Some years ago I was admitted into the "Scottish Crucible," a training path for promising young scientists based in Scotland to which I am still grateful. The trainings, and the people working there, helped me to develop a much broader view on science, and its functions, than I had at that time. It was then that I found out about the opportunities for intersection, and interaction, between scientists with no disciplinary boundaries.

In the course of one session, we were encouraged to share our knowledge beyond our academic circles. Someone said, "You are the specialists in the field. If you are not explaining to society what is happening, who is doing that?" This made me think a lot. Indeed, when something relevant happens, journalists are looking for specialists to explain to the public what is happening. When they lack this, but are still required to cover a given topic, they will have to read and process information not necessarily familiar to them in a very brief spell. Having a specialist at your disposal, in many cases, helps a lot.

I see at least three reasons to engage with public dissemination activities, that is explaining your research, or topics of your competence, to a wider public and in a nontechnical language.

1. In our work, standards are quite "wordy." Scientific papers are often 5–10.000 words. They need to be based on logic reasoning, solid evidence and a sequence that is relatively standardized. Writing 7–1.000 words with no obligation to back-up every single statement, simply saying "I think that..." may provide you with a different perspective on your work. You can use a more relaxed language and reasoning that would not always be welcome in scientific papers.

2. If you are the expert in the field on something, I think you have some sort of moral obligation to share your knowledge with the people around you and, in general, the society. If a bad decision is made and you had the knowledge to inform that decision but did not do it, it might be considered that you contributed (passively and negatively) to that bad decision. There might be no direct correlation between an article that you could have published and that decision. Nonetheless, if scientists, who study years to reach a level of knowledge well above the average, and on which a society (and a state) invests, do not speak up then who else can do it?

3. Public engagement is an excellent opportunity to become visible not only to the general public but to the scientific community itself. A few people will have time to read your long and technical articles but definitely many more have the time to read 5–600 words in a newspaper, magazine, blog or listen to your interview on the radio or TV. Being able to synthetize your work in a few words will enable you to reach a much larger audience. If a blog post is based on your academic article, and conveys the same message, then people might even claim that they have read your article and cite you and this is better than people not reading you at all or claiming to have read you but have no idea of what you are doing. I have always had the impression that my short articles are much more read than my academic articles. What has happened to me is that colleagues have contacted me asking to write a piece for them, after reading a short article of mine, something that has rarely—if ever happened—after I published a standard academic article.

Chances are that, once someone has liked your short piece, they will also decide to read a longer one that you have written. At the end of the day, people spend lots of time (officially devoted to work) looking to escape the daily grind and reading a very short article could be just that. It will not be as attractive as football or gossiping, but it is definitely more interesting than a technical academic article.

And if I still do not feel like popularizing science?

If you are not still convinced by "why you should," I could try to convince you with "why you must." Public dissemination is now a requirement by many donors. A strategy for public dissemination activities should be added to a grant application and then, if the project is funded, embedded in the contract. The donors increasingly need to show taxpayers that their money is well spent, and this has to be done by translating findings into a simple language. Besides, this can be seen also as meeting the general goal of making people more aware of the importance of science in their daily life.

In other words, if you plan a career in science, you have a little chance to escape it. You can decide whether public engagement will be a major component of your career strategy or something you will do sporadically, and possibly against your will. But it is likely that, at some point, you will have to do it. Besides, making your research public means to leave a bit of the ivory tower in which academics live. There are several excellent books that, based on solid academic findings, present research in an accessible way and provide fascinating accounts of phenomena that are not always easy to understand. Eventually, some scholars become much more successful with their public dissemination activities than scientific ones. I know of a few cases where the person getting a job in a department was not the one with the best academic records but the one with the best public dissemination capacities.

Why? Think commercially. A scientist that is often in the media makes your university more visible. When pupils need to decide into which university to enroll this might be a deciding factor. As in many other cases, there are perspective students who have a clear idea of what they want to do and where they want to go. But there is a substantial amount of school graduates who are just undecided and therefore relatively easy to convince. Having someone "famous" in your department, or school, is certainly a factor likely to help attract more students. More students mean more funding, at least in countries where funding to public universities depends on how many students enroll in a given year. Therefore, a media catalyst may be very welcome as a colleague in many departments. True that you cannot have a department of mediatic people with no one doing real research. However, a good team may be composed by people bringing different specializations and, if one of them is a media person, that might count as an asset.

Besides all the reality shows we are bombarded with, media are sometimes looking for people who can speak with authority about a given phenomenon. A university professor definitely falls within this category. They have the knowledge, the position and the authority to say things. Eventually, when you are presented on TV, few will care if you have a book with Harvard University Press or not. You will be introduced as the author of a number of books and articles on the topic and thus, someone smart and a specialist in the field. In the end, with a 2-minute appearance, you might end up becoming more visible than with any other articles you have written.

Once you are known to journalists and presenters, and you keep yourself available to appear on TV, it is relatively easy to stay in the loop and be regularly invited. But how to enter the media environment? You need to get noticed. This could be done by writing something that is seen by journalists or presenters as they are unlikely to read your academic articles (unless they are science journalists). You probably need to go their way and publish in magazines and newspapers. In some cases, someone could introduce you to the right person. When working in Germany a colleague could not attend a talk show and he gave my name to replace him. After I went I was inserted into the TV database of experts and they kept on inviting me for some time.

Why to bother with social media accounts and posting?

Academic dissemination has changed a lot recently and social media are one of the newest frontiers. I would divide them into two separate channels. One is academic social media such as academia.edu and researchgate.net. Both websites have a Facebook-like functionality allowing you to follow other scholars, getting followed, and share your works, which can also be classified into drafts, papers, books and as many categories as you want. The others are more widespread social media such as Facebook or Twitter.

Academic social media can count on a smaller, but more specialized, audience. You can be sure that 80–90% of the people you will find there are academics, wannabe academics or proto-academics. You might get fewer followers or friends than on Facebook but all of them will be, at least potentially, interested in your work. They also give you space to upload your works, your CV and anything else you might want to make public. In the end, they function a bit like your webpage with anyone being able to download any works you make public. The advantage over your webpage (the one you can have on your university's website) is that your profile can be followed, and followers receive regular updates of your work. These websites also offer an overview on your analytics and how many people read you, a thing that I find reassuring and gratifying since I am often under the impression that few, if anyone, read my works.

But in these analytics lies also the perverse risk of getting oneself pleased with what we have. On the one hand, it is useful to know that people are reading you and that they are—at least in theory—more than you feared. On the other hand, by producing for the academic world and finding your pride in being read by academics only sounds a bit alienating. Academia and ResearchGate are excellent professional websites to identify people with similar interests, to search for collaborations, spot someone in a university where you know no one. When I decided to create a collaboration with a university I had never worked with before I was able to get in touch with some colleagues through these websites. I use academia to advertise my work but also to post a call for papers, for conference participants and whatever else you need to be advertised. Using the right tagging you are likely to reach a very wide public and you can use it as a repository for material (for instance, when Tweeting about an event, you can refer to the call for papers uploaded in academia.edu). But I would not use the word "public dissemination" to refer to advertisement that you can do on these websites since the general public will barely ever use them.

The second group of websites, and social media, that you can use are Facebook and Twitter alike. Facebook has many uses, and you will always be tempted to get in touch with your old classmates or childhood friends, who have little to do with academia. But because of this, and used properly, Facebook can be an excellent crossroads between two worlds: the academic and the real one. It is unlikely that your friends will read your 10.000-word article, but nobody stops them from congratulating you for the very fact that you have a book out, an article, an interview or anything else that looks intriguing. You could also post short blog entries or thoughts and see how your public react. The same thing can be done through Twitter, that positions itself a bit more as a professional tool by default than the more eclectic Facebook. The list of media that you can use for dissemination is longer, but the principle is that you need to use different languages and approaches depending on the media. Also, there is a chance to translate your findings and professional activities into things that can be understood by larger audiences, a thing that is increasingly required by universities these days. Not all universities will put the same pressure on you to become mediatic, but some already do. In addition, being a social media star might turn out very useful to your career at some point. A friend wanted to publish a short piece on the sudden death of a despotic head of state but could not find any media outlet that would be immediately interested. He then wrote the piece and published it on the blog of his institute but widely advertised it through Facebook and Twitter. Within 3 days he received requests from the four corners of the world to elaborate his thoughts. Obviously, there was a need for articles like his, he just was not sufficiently visible. Well, not yet. Now he is and is often on TV, radio and newspapers on several continents.

Why should I try to deliver a 60-second lecture?

Academia is (slowly) modernizing. I have seen book trailers and research findings explained through a variety of artistic expressions. Personally, if I want to watch a trailer, I would go for a movie trailer. But I acknowledge that synthesizing a book in 3 minutes is a fascinating idea. Amongst the many innovative ideas that I have seen I would put a "60-second lecture" This reminds me of an exercise we did during my studies. A scientist is challenged to explain in 60 seconds a particular aspect of their research.

There are many other ways to challenge yourself, but a 60-second lecture has several advantages. First, in contrast to book trailers that require some editing skills, it can simply be a fixed camera on someone talking 60 seconds about a topic. Second, it is so short that your audience cannot get bored. Finally, it is so synthetic that you really need to train your skills to fit everything in 60 seconds.

You have to give the impression, a snapshot, of your article on which people decide if they are interested. It is not about pitching every single aspect but about showing the most salient moments of your work to convince people that it is worth their time and attention. You can use 15 seconds saying that this is your research, this is your methodology, and this is your conclusion. Eventually, it is about advertising your research.

I picked the 60-second example because it has a lot to do with our presentation skills. When you love your subject, you are able to talk for hours and hours about it and might naively assume that your public is as interested in your issue as you are. This is not always the case and keeping things short gives you more chances that people will look at them. They can then decide whether to read more of your ideas or just keep in mind that they know you. For a 60-second lecture, you need a clear strategy. You cannot afford losing a single second. You have no time but cannot try to go and speak fast and slow, you have to carefully select your words, decide what to emphasize, what to prioritize.

Well, in fact, you need a presentation strategy whatever the length of your presentation. For one minute you need to decide how to squeeze the maximum amount of information in without losing clarity. For an hour you need a way to keep people's attention at a good level, sound energetic throughout the lecture and ensure that people can follow you in most things.

There is no predefined strategy because it all depends on your presentation skills. How able you are to keep your concentration? How much you need structure not to get lost during your presentation? Or, are you able to do free-talking with little or no scheme in front of you? It also depends on the complexity of the data you are presenting. If your presentation is full of numbers, figures and facts perhaps some slides, and more structure, might help. In some cases, you might want to play a video but think whether it is worth to show a 5-minute video if you only have 15 minutes for your presentation.

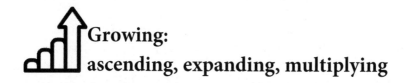 Growing:
ascending, expanding, multiplying

Is it "good" or "bad" to have co-authors?

Co-authorship is tricky. I know that some universities now ask you, in case of co-authorship, to specify what parts of the paper you have written or contributed. Some other committees will ask your co-authors to sign a statement declaring how much of an effort (30%, 50%) they have put into a paper with you as co-author so to be clear what was your contribution to a study.

I also see the fear in some of the seminar participants' eyes (usually from the humanities) when I suggest that they could co-write, or co-edit, with some other colleagues. It seems like they are afraid of sharing the merits, or purity, of their ideas and that single authorship should be the norm. On the other extreme, there is a wide amount of disciplines acknowledging that multi-authorship is a reality in academia and is, in many respects, well regulated. There are unwritten but established rules to decide on the order of authors, and negotiations to decide who should be inserted where, in a given paper.

There are several possible attitudes towards co-authorship but, in general, co-authorship is not bad per se. There is nothing bad in being the 4th or even the 99th author, especially if we are talking about a highly cited paper. But if you are always the 5th or more author in a publication then someone, at some point, might ask why you are not leading any studies.

As a bottom line, one could take the definition of an independent scholar by the European Research Council (ERC). To be eligible for an ERC grant, you need to have at least one paper not jointly written with your supervisor. I have heard of some committees minimizing merits of applicants for a paper if they are listed as the 4th (or further) co-author of a paper. I would also avoid flagging too many papers for which you are listed as the 4th or the 5th author unless you can prove that the order of authors was alphabetical.

I have two principles that I use, with some flexibility, to determine the order of authors of a paper. One is that the person in charge of the paper, to coordinate the work, identify the journal, take the lead in addressing the comments, should go as a first author. The other is that, even if I am inserted as second or later co-author in many influential papers, I should still publish at least once a year a paper of which I am the first author. In my view, the first author is the one who somehow takes the lead in the research group and going as first author demonstrates some kind of initiative, leadership skills and the capacity to remain active (or pro-active, since you bring together authors, manage them and actively look for solutions to issues that arise during the submission process).

For many people that I have met, and who come from disciplines where you claim your credits alone, co-authorship sounds exotic, at best. To some extent, I would tend to agree. If you are an anthropologist who has spent 12 months in the field and want to share your findings, and reflections, you have no room for a second, let alone third, author. But you could first publish a paper based on your novel data and then try and compare them with those by other scholars for a comparative paper. When, how and whether to engage with co-authorship is ultimately your choice. But in an academic sector where citations and h-indexes are crucial to survival, co-authorship is strategically vital to most, not to say all, of us.

As a scholar, you will have to compete with other scholars from cognate disciplines. If many of them take advantage of co-authorship to enhance their profile, then the problem is yours. You might get penalized for a fellowship, a promotion or your department might be put under pressure because it has had not "enough impact" once impact is measured, by the number of citations faculty have.

If you are in science and are used to multi-authored papers perhaps you already know it, but for the social sciences and humanities this is an open market and deserves some reflections. Think about co-authoring with 15 more colleagues and its advantages. At the very basic level, each time one of your co-authors cite themselves you earn a citation that does not count as self-citation. By contrast, if you cite yourself 15 times, it might look as you are the sole person reading yourself. For some grant applications, you are asked to provide the number of citations you attracted but exclude self-citations, which could bring the number significantly down in case few other people cite you. In addition, the more co-authors you have, the more likely it is that some of them might be more known than you and will attract citations and readership to a paper you co-authored.

I was sometimes questioned since, I was told, in the social sciences and humanities it is not a usual thing to have co-authors. But then I still remember my shock when I realized that in my department (when I was in geography) colleagues from medical geography could gather as many as 10–15 co-authors and attract hundreds of citations very quickly. And they would still be competing with other (single-authored, undercited) social scientists. I also remember a friend working in biology complaining about his low number of citations. When I went to check, he had many more than most of the people I knew, at the same career stage, in the social sciences.

How many co-authors should I take?

While in the social sciences people hesitate to take up a co-author, other disciplines have evolved to include 1000 or even 5000 co-authors. Technically speaking, if the paper has 5000 words and 1000 authors, each of the authors has, on average, written five words, or less.[3]

Of course, this is just an average measurement. In an experiment, you have people who have spent hours in a lab repeating the same process over and over again and then they shared their results. They might not have written a word but have participated in the overall process. Even with no lab experiments, you can still share tasks. If you are using models, you will need people who do simulations and other people who are able to construct a narrative to tell about these results, you might need a superstar who knows how to narrate things and to work their magic on paper. But even in an article based on qualitative work the labor can be divided: author 1 does theory, author 2 empirics, author 3 more empirics and author 4 the final polishing and editing. In a paper of 6000 words, you need to write 1500 words and you have a publication.

"Is it interesting to think so mechanically?" I was asked once. To this question I would add, is it useful and to what extent? Being author no. 967

---

[3]   Look at these threads about papers with more than 1000 authors.
A Fruit-fly paper has 1,000 authors: A Genomics paper with an unusually high number of authors sets researchers buzzing on social media.
http://www.nature.com/news/fruit-fly-paper-has-1-000-authors-1.17555
A physics paper sets a record with more than 5,000 authors
https://www.nature.com/news/physics-paper-sets-record-with-more-than-5-000-authors-1.17567

in a paper makes it unlikely that you would mention that paper in a job application or a fellowship. But it definitely increases your bibliometrics, it shows that you can work in large teams and that you have collaborated with some other established academics. It will be unlikely that someone points out the marvelous contribution of author no. 967 in that paper but when the impact is calculated you are there with a few hundred, or thousand, citations more. I do not think citations should be your reason for living but, if having too few, can land you in trouble or put your job on the line, and if you operate in a system that prizes citations, perhaps it is worth doing your homework (that is collect enough citations to stay safe in your job) before devoting yourself to what you like to do (that is, job-related things that do not necessarily bring you formal credit with your line manager, university or national evaluation system).

On whether this is interesting, I have at least two answers. One is that it might not be super interesting, but it gives you peace of mind that you have done what you were supposed to do and leaves you time, and strength, for other things. In addition, it might actually be interesting. I find sometimes working alone unmotivating, being unable to share frustrations with someone. If you get angry when you receive feedback on a paper, or if you cannot work on something one day, or feel frustrated with some part of the process, you can share it with a co-author and be sure that they will understand you because they are in the same boat. It is a bit like cycling alone or on a team. On a team, you might feel tired but keep on going because the others are going, and you do not want to be the one left behind.

In the end, if this becomes a mechanical process, then co-authorship can eventually get boring. But if you are required to survive by the market, and this means to show some achievements in the field, maybe you want to spend your time effectively while doing things you have to do so there is more time for things you want to do. If you have articles with lots of citations, then you can also write something that you like, for a non-Scopus journal, a chapter or anything just for the pleasure of writing it, even risking that no one is going to cite it.

A journal article vs a book chapter

The sharp separation between a book chapter and a journal article has not always been there and has changed throughout time. The general idea behind writing is that written production should serve to advance science and share new scientific findings but now articles and chapters are treated in a completely different way by the scholar community and national quality control institutions.

Journal articles, possibly published in journals indexed in Scopus or WoS, are the academic currency nowadays. No matter how well a book chapter might be written, a journal article will always be considered more prestigious, important, and more relevant for the advancement of scientific knowledge. This has gone so far that some disciplines, and countries, give zero credits for a book chapter published, no matter how prestigious the publisher is (i.e., Cambridge University Press).

This is, at least partly, due to a widely accepted distinction between a book chapter and an article. A book chapter could be theoretical, empirical, or both. It could also consist of notes from your fieldwork or progress findings or used to republish some of your work, be argumentative or simply descriptive. In contrast, a journal article is expected to propose a theoretical argument located in current debates on the topic you are engaging with. The argument should be innovative and based on either novel empirical data or an analysis or reinterpretation of existing studies. The article should also be original and not previously published elsewhere (not, at least, in the same language, but a translation into English of a good article published in a minor language could be acceptable by some journals).

Book chapters are much less regulated. A piece in a thematic volume, edited by one or more scholars, could consist of anything in any form as long as the editors are happy with it. In theory, a chapter should seek a dialogue with the rest of the volume and with its theoretical introduction. In practice, if the book is called "anything about something" then a chapter could take any aspect of that something and its editors could still claim coherency of the publication. Finally, book chapters need not be original. A good article could be reprinted as a book chapter, upon reprinting clearance with the journal that had initially published the article, with fewer problems than you would encounter to republish something as an article. In fact, book editors might even ask you to republish something because they find it interesting and relevant for the volume so that, with a new title, a journal article becomes a book chapter you could claim extra credit for.

Remember always to check copyright issues when planning to do this as you will need to get permission even if it is your own work. Once you have permission, you can reprint the article and even claim credits for it in some systems. However, this easy reuse of material is possibly at the origins of the fact that book chapters are less frequently used, at least in some countries, as evidence of excellent scientific production.

Why to write, or at least, publish a book chapter?

Even if not credited by your institutions, there are several reasons why you might want to publish a book chapter. Think of when you are invited to contribute a piece of a book edited by a major scholar in your field. In that case, contributing a chapter could be a chance to work with that person, learn from them and also take it as evidence that you are considered knowledgeable and reliable. There is also the case where you know that a given edited book might become the reference text for a particular topic. Think now of the increasingly popular tendency to publish "a handbook of something." If you contribute to the Handbook of International Security Studies with a chapter on Brazil, chances are that you will become "Mr. Brazil" for a number of people looking for a starting basic reference on the country in security studies.

A chapter might not count you formally towards jobs and scholarships, but it might speed up your path to wider visibility domestically and worldwide. It might also be worth keeping in mind that, while access to journal articles is usually conditional to subscription, a variety of books are available on Google Books. It is true that usually not all pages, or even chapters, are visible. However, some of your work will be accessible online and free for anyone.

I have two additional reasons that could push me to write a book chapter:

One is when I have been invited to a conference and after the organizers have proposed to work towards a collective volume. In these cases, I might want to deliver a chapter as a sign that I was happy with their hospitality and that I wish to maintain contact with them.

The other one is the freedom to publish what I want and how I want. Given that a book chapter has no standard format, I sometimes agree to deliver under the condition that the version I deliver will be the quasi-final one. The reason is practical. If I deliver a chapter and get a full peer review after which I have to spend a great deal of time rewriting it and addressing the comments I received, then why do not I just send it to a journal? The amount of work will be the same, but I will then be credited for an article, which is worth much more. If I agree to write a chapter it is because I can use it as a writing exercise, get some friendly but informal feedback and then publish some ideas that might be too unorthodox for a journal article.

A book chapter as training

Working in non-English speaking environments, I have often met scholars who, even if they could be regarded as solid good specialists, they have not been sufficiently exposed to formal training in social theory or simply have not learned the "rules of the game" of the publishing world. This has resulted, in many cases, in them being unable to place their work into well-respected academic journals. No matter how innovative their material, or how much they pay for proofreading, they have simply not understood sufficiently how to adapt their article to a Western audience. In other words, they have not learned technically how to get away with the material that they share in an article. Going an extra mile with the literature review or deepening their level of analysis might make their life easier but they have not yet met someone who took the time to explain to them how this could be done.

They might be the most famous and respected scholar in their country on the topic, but journals might not necessarily care because this is not what they want (or, even better, think their readership will not appreciate it). When working with these people I could, of course, deliver a session on how to adapt work for a Western audience. However, this requires an investment that I am not always ready to make. It takes time to organize and deliver such sessions, not everybody feels comfortable to take instructions from someone more junior than they are, some need more time to digest these suggestions and adapt their writing style.

This is why a chapter is easier for me not only to write but also to manage if I am editing something. When I see that one of my authors needs help I can take the time and explain how to technically deal with some aspects of their paper. In some cases, this goes as far as to suggest cutting the theoretical section, explain in the introduction to the chapter the linkage between the evidence presented and the topic of my edited book, and then concentrate on the empirical material and its interpretation to confirm, or challenge, the theoretical paradigm that I present in the introduction. A chapter can also be written in a free structure, so they are also easier to accept when they do not follow the classical sequence: introduction, literature, empirics, conclusion.

Why to edit a book?

In terms of credits that you can claim for editing something, a collective volume is hardly worth the efforts made. Most evaluation systems give preference to monographs or even just articles, that count much more for a promotion, fellowships or even informal credits. Getting an edited volume accepted is as hard as getting a contract for your own book. In addition, you will need to take care of 10–12 authors on average, making sure that they send their chapter on time, provide feedback, listen to their moaning when needed. Sometimes you will have to make painful decisions, such as rejecting a chapter or excluding an author that is particularly indolent. Finally, you will have to write an introduction, a conclusion and possibly contribute to a chapter yourself. A few more chapters and you could actually write a monograph and claim credits for it.

Still, in some disciplines, there is still an understanding that an edited book is needed at some point in one's career. I would guess the reasons are at least twofold: you have to demonstrate some management skills and to be able to build a small network (or already have a hold on a network) on a topic of your choice.

Despite the few credits to be earned, an edited book offers, at least in my view, a minimum of four advantages.

First, it is a chance to write a theoretical chapter providing a broad overview on the topic (usually the introduction) that would have no room elsewhere. The only alternative would be the introductory chapter in your own monograph but that takes much more time and effort. In addition, you can build your introduction with the support of evidence from a variety of empirical cases provided by the contributors, a thing that may strengthen your argument. It is true that introductions are much less visible than books.

But I have in my mind a few introductory chapters that are extremely well cited and known and are now a reference on their topic.

Second, it is a chance to deliver a piece on a topic that is theoretically, empirically and geographically broader than what you would be able to deliver alone. A monograph can go much deeper, but an edited book goes wider and this is also important, not least to show that your topic is of global relevance.

Third, it is a bonding exercise. By working with 10–12 authors, some of which you did not know in the beginning of the process, you create a link between you and them that is likely to bring long-term collaborations with at least some of them. Once you are the author who brought the concept of the book to life, and the introduction bringing together all the chapters, authors will have to interact, read some of your work, ask for suggestions, receive feedback and work as a team on some tasks. This is an exercise, which brings you closer to each other (even if sometimes it ends up in fights with one or more of the authors) and possibly leads them to get more acquainted with your work, which in turn can mean more citations and possible future collaborations (invitations into projects, guest lectures and publications).

Fourth, it is a low labor intense process (if compared to a monograph) to show to the academic community that you are an active researcher. The fact that it requires less work than a monograph does not mean, automatically, that it is easier or less stressful. In the end, it all depends on your management skills. If you are someone able to work long hours alone, then you might be more apt to write a monograph than to edit a book. Ultimately, the difference might not be in the number of hours but in the way they are distributed. An edited book requires regular interaction with authors to provide feedback and to solve day-to-day management issues that are unlikely to occur when you prepare a monograph.

Much of these downsides of editing can be mitigated, or even avoided, by dividing the work. If you are not the sole editor, tasks can be shared or divided. Single authorship is an odd fetish in the social sciences so much so that I have seen people not admitting a second or third co-editor for fear that their merits would dwindle. But for an edited collection, that is already worth close to zero in terms of formal credits, how much of your credit can you lose when editing alone? And how many of your nerves can you save?

Working with someone is not only a bonding experience but can allow you to work at different paces. Today I am unable to work for personal or professional issues and you work more. But tomorrow you have your own issues and I make up for them by working a bit more for you as you did yesterday for me. It is a way to divide tasks, have to review fewer chapters (or having a second or third opinion on each chapter), take advantage of different specializations of each of the co-editors. One of you could be stronger on theory, another could be an English native speaker and help with copy-editing, another might be an excellent (or at least wannabe) manager and handle the communication with the authors. I have little motivation to go through this alone but edited books have allowed me to stir a dialogue with the academic community and remain visible even when I have had no time to prepare my own monograph.

Why to edit a special issue of a journal?

The considerations shared for an edited book also apply to a guest-edited issue of an academic journal with two additional tangible advantages. Less work is required, and it gets you more credit formally.

First, a special issue of a journal usually hosts 4–8 papers. This might include a guest editorial and your own article. Managing 6–8 authors is less time consuming than 10–12. There are also no conclusions to be written, no index and, when editing a special issue, you get some support from the journal's regular editor, and managing an editorial team, who are interested in ensuring that your special issue maintains the same level of quality as the journal and satisfies its readers.

Second, there is definitely more credit to be gathered. A journal article counts more than a chapter in an edited book in most evaluation systems. In addition, as a guest editor you have an agency on the review process and, even if in theory your paper will be peer-reviewed, you can, in fact, contribute identifying reviewers that are constructive and will do their job quickly. In other words, you can induce a best-case scenario for the review of your own paper (see the question on the agency of a journal editor). Finally, many journals have tended to a model treating the editorial (the short introductory piece introducing the issue) as an article. As a result, as an author of the editorial and of an article you will be able to claim authorship of two pieces, rather than one. True that only one is a real article and the other has to be checked, but in a world dominated by bibliometrics and automatic classifications of academic outputs few will stop and reflect on this. Eventually, when encoding your academic output your results will be counted as author, or co-author, of two academic articles instead of an editorial and an article.

In many respects, a special issue is definitely more convenient than an edited book. Add to this that a special issue sometimes can also be republished as an edited book and you have killed two birds with one stone. However, there is a hidden cost making guest special issues difficult to access.

Where an edited book follows a standard procedure, known to most academics, of submitting a proposal, getting a contract, delivering and getting published; a special issue of a journal has a less standardized path. For one thing, it is unclear where to send a proposal to apply for a special issue. Not all journals allow guest-edited issues and, of those who do, only a few openly advertise them. Most journals are in principle open to special issues but allow them only on demand, if someone whom they trust proposes something that the editorial board is willing to invest in. In other words, being given the steering wheel of a journal for a while is a matter of personal connections. It depends on your reputation, how well you know the journal editor and how solid your proposal is. Ultimately, an editorial team will give you a special issue if they think they will gain something from you. That could be visibility, cover a topic that nobody else wants to cover but is nonetheless important, the fact that you are bringing top scholars to write for that journal, and/or propose something innovative. There are no limits to this and it ultimately depends on how visible and famous a journal already is, but they have to see you as an added value rather than them thinking to be doing you a favor.

Why to publish with an academic press?

While, in some countries, a book is considered of high quality as long as it is published with a major publisher, in evaluation systems that are very selective academic presses are better ranked than commercial publishers (Springer, Taylor and Francis). I refer to them as academic presses because they are based at some university and can, accordingly, publish under the name of that university. But academic presses may be run according to the same business model used by what I refer to as commercial publishers here.

It is also worth keeping in mind that not all academic presses offer the same level of quality or are regarded as having the same status in different classification systems. However, the general perception in academia is that certain university presses are highly selective and guarantee higher quality standards than the rest. The most exclusive classification of publishers that I have seen so far was in Hong Kong, where only the cream of the cream of academic presses (Cambridge, Harvard, Oxford etc.) would get you full credit. Other reputable ones are still worth one's attention, but they are not classified as an A+ but simply as an A.[4]

There are several factors to consider when choosing an outlet for your work:

1. **Timing vs quality**: the feedback you receive on your proposal, and then manuscript, varies. It goes from "it's publishable" to detailed comments and suggestions on the proposal, and then the final text. Presses wishing to keep their reputation solid, and concerned about quality, will also be more demanding and require more work, perform several rounds of review and recheck the manuscript several times. As a result, the time lapse between your proposal submission and publication will be longer with some presses (usually academic ones). On the bright side, once you are reviewed several times and have worked more on a manuscript that eventually gets published, it is more likely that your book will be of good quality and will also be perceived as such. Prestige of a press counts in academia and even the sole mention of a book with a major publisher has an impact on your CV and how people, and potential employers, will look at you.

2. **Price, and pricing**, policy: would you want to write the book of your life, and put several years of your life into a project, to discover that it is accessible only to an elite group of students and scholars because it is too pricey? Science books are usually more expensive than novels but how much more depends on the price policy of the publisher. Some publishers will go for a hardback only, pricing it at over €100. Some others will issue the paperback and hardback at the same time. E-books are now a reality and are sold cheaper, even if some people (including myself) will still tell you that holding a book in your hands is a different story. I have recently seen options like "access for 6 months or for a year" at a fraction of the original

---

[4]   See http://www.cityu.edu.hk/scm/pbpr_roa/PBPR%20Final%20Draft.pdf

price. Before deciding on a publisher, thus, it might be worth checking their price policy to ensure that you agree with it.

3. **Perceived quality**: even if you are absolutely sure of the quality of your work, know how many hours you have spent polishing, checking and editing everything, there is no guarantee that other scholars will perceive it in the same way. Even worse, there is no guarantee that in your national evaluation system, the book you have worked on for years will get you the credits you believe you deserve. As a general rule, the best presses are the best everywhere. I cannot imagine anyone objecting that Harvard University Press "...yes, they publish some decent stuff but, still..." No matter how criticized a book gets, it is still Harvard. There are a number of others on a more volatile standing. Some might be considered of low quality by a great majority of academics but still be prized at the national level. Some others might be of variable quality, for instance, have some series edited by scholars with a first-class reputation and who work a lot to deliver quality and other ones that are somehow abandoned intellectually.

Case study: classification of a publisher

In many respects, pressure to classify academic publishers is lower than the one to classify and rank journals. Whilst there is Scopus, WoS and ERIH for journals and they can be taken as starting points internationally, there is nothing equivalent for book publishers. Classification is rather done at the domestic level and differs from country to country. I know only three ways of ranking academic publishers: centralized, bottom-up and "in or out."

Centralized: a national committee agrees on a series of rules allowing to distinguish a "good" press from others. The distinctive trait here is that an independent committee of experts is created and interacts directly with the ministry or the quality assurance organ. The most likely drawback is that the list is either very exclusive or, based on some quantitative criteria, comes to include also some dubious mid and low-range publishers.

Bottom-up: universities, or departments, are requested to produce a list of publishers that they consider to be the top ones. Departments may then consult their own staff asking to produce a list of publishers that they

---

believe are the best in their field. The aggregate of these lists then becomes the main list used by the ministry to set the boundary between first class publishers and the others. The main drawback with this approach is that each member of a department will provide a list of publishers that they consider the best in their discipline but also including the ones they have published with. Would you do otherwise? You are asked to provide a list of best publishers and you leave out some you have published with. How would you justify the fact that you have consciously chosen to publish with a second or low-class publisher? How many people would be brave enough to declare this openly? The final list will thus include some of the best publishers along with ones that are there just because someone in the department has published with them. Some publishers have a varied reputation across disciplines, and book series, but this will not be specified since the list of the best book publishers is usually prepared nationally for all disciplines together.

In or out: this usually happens in systems with little resources to classify and with a relatively young science sector. If the country has little tradition of international academic excellence or has had few exchanges with the rest of the world, then a "good publisher" will be virtually any "international publisher" meaning they are located outside the country and publish in English. This approach is the easiest one to manipulate since, in theory, makes it possible to claim credit for any book published with any notorious or suspicious publisher as long as it sounds exotic and academic. However, as easy as it might be to get recognition at the bureaucratic level, there are several publishers that you do not want to have on your CV if you apply for an international fellowship.

What can I expect from a commercial publisher?

A number of commercial publishers have some quality control. The books they produce belong in thematic series, or series covering a geographic area and usually they have an academic as a series editor. The fact that an academic will be consulted when deciding whether to accept a book proposal is in line with accepted academic standards. Proposals will be, in principle, peer-reviewed.

However, academics are humans, they have their own preferences, idiosyncrasies and, most important, do not have the same quality standards. Inasmuch as uncomfortable this may sound, that you may have "better" and "worse" academics at your university, or your series, this variable academic quality is the ultimate reason why university, departments and scholars are scrutinized and regularly assessed against some (sometimes dubious) criteria.

In addition to this, commercial publishers, and publishers in general, will be more interested in publishing something that they feel they can sell more widely. Profit is in the manifesto of anyone operating in a market environment. But even if you take the most non-profit oriented entity, higher revenues from a book means more money to be invested in other projects or activities, a thing that is highly desirable.

Book proposals will be assessed, internally, externally or both, against a number of criteria. Academic quality may be one of them. But, in the review form, there are also questions about the market potential. Eventually, a well-written book with little market potential might be turned down and a poorly written one with good market potential might be accepted. A colleague once shared the feedback he had received from a commercial publisher that read, "Quality is low, but the book will sell. We will take it." I cannot imagine the book to be really terrible, but this anecdote tells a lot about some attitudes that you might encounter on your way.

I came across a similar situation with an article. I was doing the initial editorial screening of articles before choosing the reviewers and one of the articles we had received seemed very weak to me. The author, in some parts of the article, claimed to be a senior scholar of high resonance in the community. I decided to read up on who the author was and found out he was someone at some advanced career stage with at least a book with a major commercial publisher. How could a person, capable to publish with a major publisher, write such an article?

I went to check out the book and found it weak, superficial and in general written with little rigor. How did he make it through then? My guess, which remains a guess but on which I am quite confident, is that he had proposed to write a book on a topic that was fancy at that time and that he offered to cover a country on which nothing else had been written. The market value of the book was high, regardless of the quality he would eventually deliver. So, the publisher's decision was to "take it."

On the other side of the spectrum, commercial publishers could reject a good book on the grounds that it was not marketable. I sent a proposal to a commission editor that I knew, and he said that he was sorry, but the book had little perspective to sell so they had to turn it down. I contacted the editor of another series with another publisher and he was happy to endorse the project. We went into production and, by the time the book was printed, the publisher had been acquired by the first publisher, so we eventually edited the book for the publisher that had rejected us. Even more paradoxical, that book has brought me the highest amount of royalties I have ever received so far.

Why to publish a book that sells at €150 per copy?

One of my last books was initially sold at €150 per copy before being priced down to €120. The scary thing is that to me it sounds completely normal. Not only, I have convinced myself that academic books must be expensive. But I have also come to know, and endorse, a business model keeping prices and targeting solely (Western) libraries (who else can afford such prices?).

I have tried to move away from this model for several reasons. First, I do not see why there should be so much disbalance in income. I do not need to be paid for my books since I am already paid for my research, but I do not see why someone else, usually a large corporation, should make money on my work so that I get the glory and they get the earnings. Second, I do not see why most people on the planet should be unable to access my work since it gets protected by copyright and I am not even authorized to share it publicly.

Yet, there are several reasons why I am still stuck with this model and keep on working with a number of usual publishers that basically monopolize the academic the market.

First, it is now easy for me to publish with them. Once you have an ongoing relationship with one of these companies they will be easy to deal with and, once you are sufficiently established, they will easily take a manuscript from you. I once needed to get a book contract quickly and negotiated the speed at which I would be able to get feedback and eventually signed the contract.

It all went smoothly, and we all got what we wanted. The publisher got a book that would sell, and I got the contract I needed as a project deliverable.

Second, they are credited in most countries at the same level. On the prestige market of academia, nothing compares to presses that are in the Olympus of academic publishers (i.e., Cambridge, Yale, Princeton, Oxford, Harvard). But some commercial publishers come, in many countries, immediately after them. Academia moves slowly, once you have earned a reputation it will be difficult to lose it unless you really screw it up somehow. As a result, a number of commercial publishers bring you enough credits to deserve to be included in your survival strategy. Publishing with Oxford or Cambridge is definitely better, but the additional effort required is simply not worth the investment, at least as I see it for my personal survival strategy.

Finally, a number of independent publishers, that may have a good reputation in some countries and worse in others, do not really sell at a much lower price and do not necessarily give you better service in terms of assistance or support. As a result, you might put into a book a great deal of effort and not be credited the way you expected or needed to be. Some commercial publishers, by contrast, bear some kind of guarantee labels and sometimes have series editors with excellent reputations. Some of them are also people whom I look up to.

That said, my strategy is composed of two parts. If I write something to claim formal credit for it, I do not care at what price it will be sold at since I need it to survive and gain visibility. After all, I can always share drafts of my book privately with whoever asks for it. It will not be as nice as holding the paper book, but the content is there. However, if I write something because I want people to read it widely, my preference would go to a publisher that will guarantee some quality with a minimal price. Before finding ibidem, who agreed to sell this book at a minimal price, I was ready to simply publish the Scopus Diaries as a PDF book and even pay for an ISBN number myself in order to maximize its dissemination potential.

I have sent a book proposal to a publisher. Why did I not get any feedback?

I answer the above question with another question. How many book proposals do you think an editor of a decent publisher receives every day?

Do not limit your count only to sane people, think how many wannabe academics there are. It is unbelievable but there are many more than you think. Think also of how many people have an academic job but have more ambitions than time and they shoot too high for the quality they are going to offer. I start from the assumption that anyone can deliver quality; but quality takes time, and this depends on how fast you metabolize comments, how self-critical you are and other factors. But, at any rate, not everyone has time so different people, at different stages of their professional careers, deliver different quality.

Add, to this, crazy people thinking "Oh my book is just fantastic as it is, the world will eventually understand my genius," or "My work is going to bring a revolution to science." It is a dream of many, but sometimes people get caught up in their dreams to the point that they lose their critical skills. In other words, there are people from all over the world waiting to become famous, or get academic recognition, a higher salary, or a better reputation in their department. Once they have a manuscript ready, they might want to send it to the same academic publisher that you chose for yourself. This increases the number of submissions an editor receives and decreases the time they have at their disposal to take care of your proposal.

I would fairly assume that a majority of editors receive more proposals than they can process. And they have many other things to do apart from reading proposals. Some are full-time academics some others have marketing or promotion tasks. They also need to follow, to a certain stage, the production of the books that they have accepted. They have meetings, urgencies, families, holidays and many other things. The time devoted to looking through proposals is not as much as one might think so that you might need to work to make your proposal noticed. In addition, just like it happens with journal articles, sending a proposal for external review has a cost, not only economic (since feedback on proposals is usually paid): you have to identify a reviewer and ask them to do a review and, once this done, you will not be able to call upon that person for some time.

Finally, as a reviewer, if I receive a very bad proposal to review, I might think that the editor does not screen their proposals seriously enough. As an editor, you do not want your reviewer to think that you allow low-quality proposals to pass as this might affect your reputation. And reputation, in academia, is most of the capital you have. Some small publishers who do not get enough proposals will read it attentively and give you feedback. On the contrary, some major publishers receive just way too many proposals, will just think "I have 10 better ones, or at least with a better selling potential, than this one," and reject your proposal at once, or simply forget to answer.

Case: book contract to a junior vs a senior scholar

When you apply for a job, a number of potential employers will tell you that you need to have previous experience. But if everybody is looking for someone with previous experience and you do not have any how can you gain previous experience? This is a major entry barrier to the job market. Likewise, fewer publishers are willing to give a book contract to someone who has never published one before. How to find an entry point?

Some years ago, I had to go through this kind of initiation. I had an idea for a book and I asked a friend if he wanted to collaborate on it together, since it is more fun, and easier, to work with someone. We worked on the concept and I approached a few commission editors at a conference I attended. One of them seemed interested so she gave me her business card and asked to see a proposal. We exchanged a few emails and discussed the project but, in her last message, she said something like "I do not feel confident to give a contract to two junior scholars who have never published a book before. I suggest that you publish more and then get back to me with your proposal."

That was upsetting, how could we publish more if we were not given a chance to do so? At any rate, we digested the answer and went on with our (academic) lives. We published a special issue on the topic, a couple of more articles and, meanwhile, we contacted another publisher. We did not receive any answer for several months, so I decided to contact the first publisher again, the one that had initially rejected us, and for some reason, they decided to give us a contract. Had the topic gotten hotter and more timely? Were they impressed by our achievements from the past six months? We will probably never know. But the interesting thing was that, the week we had to send the signed contract to the publisher, the second publisher also contacted us.

For some reason or another, of which we will also never know, they had finally seen our email and became interested in our proposal. They went as far as to ask for a phone call (by default, all the previous communication had happened through e-mail) during which they asked us not to sign the contract with the first publisher and to go with them.

We went back to the first publisher and candidly explained that, because the second one was more prestigious, and we had the option of publishing with either, we would rather turn them down and go with the second. I cannot deny that we experienced some sort of satisfaction while rejecting those who had rejected us in the first place, but we made sure our message was polite and neutral though. The first publisher said that they were aware of their ranking and that the second one would bring, yes, an extra ounce of prestige.

From that moment I am on the fast track with the second publisher. I am "white-listed," meaning that my e-mails will be answered, and my proposals given full consideration. I might still get a no, for instance, if the editor thinks that my project is not financially viable, but I can also negotiate things such as the speed at which I will receive a contract.

How to maximize the chances that you will get a (hopefully positive) reply from a publisher?

You might be one of the brightest scholars in your field but, like everywhere else, you need this to be acknowledged by the gatekeepers if you want to sell your work. Scientists that emerge quickly often have worked with some established scholars and this can be ascribed to two reasons.

The first one is that you are more likely to get meaningful suggestions, and learn a lot and quickly, when working with someone who is an excellent scholar. To this one could add the assumption that excellent scholars tend to choose excellent younger collaborators, which is not necessarily accurate. I usually choose, to work with, the people who suit me the most according to the values and priorities that I have at that given moment. What suits me and what suits the system do not necessarily overlap all the time.

The second, and much simpler, is that if someone famous tells you that something is good, you are much easier to convince than if an anonymous stranger, or someone you do not look up to, tells you the same thing. This is a basic rule of marketing, according to which companies pay football players millions to claim that they are using a given product and academia is no exception. You have friends, colleagues you trust, people you admire. If one of your gurus tells you to read one of their student's work you will do it, or at least claim to have done it. You might want to keep their works into account and also avoid criticizing them too much since you might be indirectly criticizing your guru. This might be done also through a personal network, introducing your student into your circles and giving them access to people around you, which is considered the usual praxis in academia.

So, to maximize your chances to receive a positive answer you need to have some kind of connection with a publisher. This could happen through someone who introduces you to the publisher or by meeting the publisher at some conference. The higher ranked the publisher the better the connection must be to be given consideration. There are mid-low range publishers that will contact you directly even when you are a junior scholar. You might happen to just announce the program of a conference, or your PhD defense, and some publishers will write asking you to consider publishing the conference papers, or your dissertation, with them.

What are the entry points to approach a publisher?

I do not rule out that you might get lucky and receive a positive answer when writing to a top publisher. But the project might be much smoother, shorter or easier, if you have an entry point and there are two main ways to get one: to work with someone who has already published with them or to establish a rapport with someone who has a role in the publication processes.

You could co-edit or co-write with someone who has already published with that publisher. In that case, you let them make the first steps: contact the editor and agree on a contract. But after you publish with them, you are in. You can then always go by yourself to the publisher and say, "I am one of your authors."

You could also just get to know someone with a role in the production process. That could be a fellow scientist who is acting as a series editor. Once you have been endorsed by the series editor, the publisher is more likely to take your proposal into consideration. You might even discover that you know the series editor already or meet them at an international event. True that, to endorse you, they need to like your work but what is also true is that to like your work they need to read it, and they already have a lot to read without your work. But once they know you as an individual, and find you a pleasant person, or simply have the impression that you are a serious scholar and do some interesting work, they are more likely to like you work. Or simply to assume that they would like your work if they read it, so it is worth the effort to endorse you.

The same could also be done with someone working for a publisher and who has some degree of agency in the selection and commissioning of books. The better they know and like you, the stronger they will support the publication of your work. Of course, they might get vetoed or questioned at a board meeting, but this is definitely a stronger starting point than just sending your proposal to the general manuscript submission address.

Where to meet them? Publishers usually send some representatives to academic conferences. The better the conference the more likely that the best publishers will be there. The higher level the conference the higher the level (and decisional power) of the representative that will be sent there. If you choose your conference well, you are likely to meet the publishers you might want to approach. And if you can go to several conferences you will be able to construct a rapport with them faster. Alternatively, if you do not have time or money to attend conferences, you can simply check the website and see who the publisher's representative is with similar interests as yours. The closer your interests are to their personal and professional ones, the more they might be willing to recommend your work, and thus expand the focus of the publisher into a direction that they fancy and enjoy.

How to increase the chances that your proposal will be ignored?

It is true that giving someone a book contract does not mean that you will marry or hire that person. You offer a service in exchange for work and they offer their work in exchange for the service you offer. But there are elements, other than what is written in a CV and a proposal, that eventually have a role on whether your proposal will be considered. What is equally important is, what mood the person who will screen and send it for review will be in when they get your message.

The three fundamental messages that an editor can include, in a more or less explicit form, when sending a proposal for review are:

- o Please review, I have no strong opinion on this (quality or topic wise).
- o Please review, I think it is good (or it will sell well) and we would like to publish it, but we still need an external review (possibly by someone whose expertise is on this very topic) to comply with peer review expectations (and anyway taking a second look at it will not harm it).
- o Please review, I (or we) do not really like it (or think it is not good) but I cannot just reject it altogether by myself as we have a policy to peer review, anyways, all proposals.

What is important to keep in mind is that attitude towards a proposal, or an author, is only partly depending on the quality of their proposal. An editor offering you a contract commits to work with you for some months. But editors are humans. The more unpleasant communication with you is, the more they will try avoiding working with you. After all, who willingly accepts tasks that bring them extra stress? Of course, if you are not the tidiest author ever but you compensate this by being nice and regular in your communication that might help. Also, I am not talking here of rejecting an excellent proposal but, if an editor has to choose from two equally decent ones, good or bad communication dynamics, or personal chemistry with one of the authors might be the straw that breaks the camel's back.

In the end, it all depends on how much an editor can take, how stressed or busy they are, but the more they like you the more likely they will be willing to work with you (and vice versa).

Other reasons that may push them to minimize interactions with you could be:

Poor communication skills: think of when you receive an email with no subject, when they spell your name wrongly or, in general, when you do not understand what the person wants after reading a sentence. This includes when you send a message with no title or titled "book proposal" or "application for the position." What if I am responsible for several positions or book proposals? How can I know what you are applying for? Sometimes I receive emails like, "This is my application for summer school," and I wonder which one (how can that person be sure that I am not organizing more than one summer school at the same time? Such a title reads almost like spam.

Unprofessional attitude: you are often late with replies, or write on time but too much, asking them to solve problems that you should be dealing with by yourself, or you send some incomplete drafts expecting that someone will do (some of) your job.

Arrogance or pretentiousness: you claim, or sound to be, much more important than you are, that you have no time because you have many things to do (don't we all?). I would insert in this cluster also conceiving the coolest titles that claim to solve all the problems of the world. I had a colleague extremely skilled at writing catchy, long and unintelligible titles. I find this an excellent strategy to make someone feel stupid, which is not necessarily what you might want to achieve. First, someone might get upset with you because they feel stupid because of you. But, even worse, someone a bit more self-confident might question the use of these words and consider that you are trying to sound smarter than you are.

Fast and famous: publisher's vs author's reputation

Not everyone can publish with Harvard University Press. But not everybody wants to. The reason you might want to get a book with a major publisher is relatively simple. But why would someone decide not to try to publish with a major press? There are several reasons that I can imagine.

The simplest one is, of course, that someone thinks they will never make it into it. I will not discuss here whether this is lack of self-esteem, confidence or simply realistic expectations knowing the level (or just focus) of one's work. It could be a mix of the three.

But there are cases in which an author decides, in full conscience, that they want to go for a mid or low range publisher. This was the case of an American emeritus professor who wrote a good book that was allegedly not marketable and all major publishers he contacted declined to publish it. He was not concerned with fame or obsessed by ranking. He was retired and had little to prove to anyone. But he wanted his work to be read so he published it on his own. It turned out that there was no other book on the same topic so, in the end, an unexpectedly large number of libraries ordered it.

In a similar fashion, you might want that your work, and the long hours spent working on something, simply to see the light of day and become available to a large audience. Now, if you want a position in a top university, not going with a famous publisher might be a problem (unless you intend to hide the publication when you apply for the position). But if you are content with just having a manuscript then you could potentially go with anything. The bottom line is, in my view, two-fold. First, whatever publisher you go with, make sure that they have a good copy-editing process or, at least, that your manuscript is free from typos and mistakes. Not being able to enjoy your reading because of technical imperfections is one of the greatest sins in academia and the publishing industry in general. Second, try to avoid publishers that are considered as a "vanity press" or "predatory" ones. They will not only add a zero to your CV but actually shed a shadow on it.

My question when I see someone who published with a notorious press would be: did the person go with them because they have radical, unusual, alternative opinions that mainstream publishers will not consider worth the effort of publishing or because that author delivered such a low quality of work that they could not go anywhere else? I was once screening CVs for a position and a colleague wanted to share one that he was impressed with. He said, "Have you seen this? He has a PhD, 2 books and 5–6 articles." I was somehow suspicious, so I went to check out some of the journals and I found out that, in spite of their serious and professional looking title, these were not well-reputed journals and some, not to say all, did not perform any peer reviews and published for a fee.

All other options for publishing are fine but the more junior you are, the more you need recognition, and thus the more you need endorsements. Publishing with a good publisher means you are endorsed by that publisher that guarantees the quality of your work. However, the more you advance in your career, the more the equation gets reversed. It is you who gives legitimacy to a publisher who, having you amongst their authors, increases their visibility and prestige. This is the usual path also if you need to launch something new (a book series, a journal). If you ask famous academics to write an article for your journal, you can offer little in terms of recognition or prestige, but if they endorse your project and write for you. Now, having the top scientists publishing with you means that they believe in your project, making it more likely that people will notice the project and that it will grow fast and famous.

Journal ranking and other academic obsessions (slow and fast journals)

The ranking of a journal depends on its Impact Factor (IF), which basically depends on the number of citations that the articles contained in that journal manage to attract. Given that the number of citations you can expect for an article dramatically vary across disciplines, I usually suggest that there are "fast" and "slow" disciplines. To distinguish fast from slow I refer here to the speed an article is published and cited. Let me share two vignettes that I use during my workshops.

Imagine a philosopher sitting on the grass under a tree and deeply philosophizing. After some thousand hours of free and unrestricted thinking, our philosopher comes up with an idea that is then turned into an extremely dense article of 10,000 words. Philosophers do not usually use a formula but may have a lot to say. They write, polish, then edit and polish again and, finally, after a number of months spent on the article, submit it to a peer review journal. The editor likes the article and sends it to two reviewers who also like it. But because it is a long article and they want their comments to be detailed they will take some weeks, not to say months, to send their comments back to the editor, who will forward them to the author.

The author will read them and start digesting them, then amend the article accordingly and prepare an answer to explain how some of them were addressed, some were not and why, and what has been changed.

Depending on the journal's policy, the editor might organize a further round of reviews, or screen the article and ask for some amendments to be made, after which the article is accepted, and published. Once published, other scientists will read the article and decide perhaps to respond, criticize it, or simply cite it as one of the works on the topic. Someone else, thus, will start working on an article and undergo the process above after which, all going well, the original author will get a citation.

Given that the turnover, from submission to acceptance, is usually 12–24 months, this may mean:

- o Write the article in 2013
- o Submit it in 2013
- o Get it accepted in 2014 (or 2015)
- o Someone reads it in 2015 and decides to cite it
- o They submit it in 2016
- o It is accepted in 2017–2018

Chances are that, by these calculations, the philosopher above will get their first citations after five years. Now, you can have journals that have a faster turnover, shorter articles, quicker reviewers. You can also share your draft or unpublished manuscript at conferences so to attract citations for your conference presentation already (which will be named just like the article, so you can then hijack citations from the conference paper to the article). But this is more or less the path. After a certain number of articles, you will start attracting citations faster but with a 2–4 year delay (citations you gather this year are most likely from articles you have written 2–3 years ago), unless you are a superstar and people live waiting for your next article to cite it.

Now, think of a lab scientist. They are likely to work with a team of other scientists who do experiments over some weeks, or months, after which a paper is prepared and published. There is no standard timing for experiments, it could be a week or a year, but there are some features that make citations grow faster. First, even if the main difficulty is to come up with calculations and a formula that explains your experiments, once these are done you can publish more than one paper resulting from the same experiment. Second, papers are significantly shorter (3–5000 words). They thus require less time to be written, polished and even reviewed. The formula has to be checked and the methodology can still be criticized but the turnover will be faster. Finally, articles are multi-authored so that even undergraduate students might be listed as authors, and thus gather citations before their master's degree or PhD. It also means that, once the article is submitted, it will attract citations from any of the followers of any of the authors of the paper. If there are 100 authors, the paper will be much more visible than if it had only one author.

So, taking the above path, chances are that the article is prepared quickly after the experiment is finished (that could have lasted 3 weeks) and it receives reviews within a few weeks. All going well, it will come out within a few months (and in the same year). Other scholars who want to cite it and criticize it might be able to prepare the counter-experiment and eventually write the article also very quickly. In addition, the article will be shared with their contacts and by all of the various authors. Finally, for an article co-authored by 100 scientists, if each of the authors simply cites themselves in their next article, the current article will already have 100 citations.

These are ideal situations at the extreme end of the spectrum and citation levels, regardless of the field, it still depends on the quality of the paper and the reputation of the authors. But the above examples can give you an idea of what may happen in a best and worst-case scenario. A journal is nothing but an aggregate of articles so, once most of them start being cited, as happens for hard science articles, the journal's citations shoot up. As a result, the difference between a humanities journal and a science one might be quite substantial in terms of article turnover and citation potential.

This is why I distinguish "fast" journals, that publish and gather citations quickly, and "slow" journals, that are cited in a more sporadic and irregular way. You can also guess, at this stage, why some journals have an impact factor of 30 and some others of 0.2. But this is also why the impact factor of a journal tells you little unless you explain in which discipline you are. In the humanities 1 is already a pretty good IF whereas in astrophysics 1 would mean that your journal is barely cited, at least compared to others in the same discipline.

Which Scopus quartile is the ideal one for you?

A given sampled population (people, animals, journals), once ranked according to some pre-defined criteria, can be divided into quartiles, each of which contains 25% of the total sample population.

In a sample of 1000 journals, ranked by IF, each quartile contains 250 journals. So, allegedly, being in Q1 means you are among the top 25% of academic journals in the world, being in Q2 means that your journal is in the second top 25% (thus amongst the best 50% of journals in the world). If your journal is in Q3, it means that it belongs in the top 75% of journals in the world. Q4 means that you are in the top 100% of journals, which basically means little, except for the fact that you are included in a database, a thing that sometimes counts already.

The impact factor of a journal is calculated on the basis of the number of citations for two years divided by the number of citable documents published in these same two years. In practice, it measures how many times on average an article, published in a given journal, is cited over a given period. If each published article of a given year is cited, on average, at least once then the journal has an IF of 1. The number is higher if there are more citations per article, it is lower if there are fewer.

There are situations where the last journal in Q1 has 0.461 and the first in Q2 has 0.451. This means, at least to me, that the two journals have a de facto of the same impact factor. But one is considered to be in the top 25% in the world and the other only in the top 50%. In a system that gives you credits for any Scopus article, this difference is not very important. But some systems give more credit for a Q1 publication than for a Q2 so, in such cases, it is important to keep in mind that not all Q1 publications are a de facto Q1 for you. The impact factor is calculated each year and the last article in Q1 has more chances to fall into Q2 than other ones. If you target the last article in Q1 and, by the time your article is published, the journal's impact factor has fallen from 0.461 to 0.449 you might not be in the position to claim Q1-credit for that article.

Some universities or evaluation systems prize Q1 articles more than Q2, Q3, Q4. Some other systems simply prize any article in a Scopus journal regardless of it being in Q1 or Q4. It is your job to learn what is the optimal output for the country you are working in. Obviously, publishing in a Q1 journal is always better than publishing in Q2, Q3 or Q4. The question is how much added value will you get for a Q1 article if compared to a Q4 publication. If you virtually get the same amount of credit, then is it worth the effort? Q1 journals might be harder to get in but they give you more visibility. But if you are trying to save your job (for instance, you need to publish something quickly in a Scopus journal) perhaps you could target anything indexed in that database, save your back and only after that think about your glory.

In some systems, they give the same credit for an article in a Scopus or in an ISI journal, but ISI is less inclusive, so it might be more difficult to get it in there. In some other systems, they also include the ERIH (European Reference Index for Humanities) database, where I have noticed the presence of journals that are not peer-reviewed.

In the end in which journal, quartile and database to publish in is a result of your calculations based on:

what you need to do (to keep your job, fulfill your plan)

what you are expected to do (by your line manager, maybe they want you to become the leader of the research group, or to apply for a professorship, and you need to have excellent articles)

what you want to do (your personal ambitions)

how easily you can get there (how hard it is to get into Q1 or, in general, a given journal).

Why a journal may rank in different quartiles for different disciplines in Scopus

When delivering a workshop, I ask participants to suggest a name of a journal so to construct a case study from a discipline they feel confident in. During a session, I was suggested "Mortality." Not the happiest name ever but it can make an interesting case. To check the status of a journal one could enter the official Scopus website (https://www.Scopus.com) or, if you have no institutional access, simply go to Scimago (www.scimagojr.com). This website uses the same software and similar features but needs no login. It has a 12-month embargo so that you will not have access to the latest information. For instance, if a journal has been admitted into Scopus less than 12 months ago, or has changed quartile in the past 12 months, you will not be able to see it.

However, given the speed at which academia moves, 12 months is not a very long period, you will still be able to see the general tendencies and understand what the international status of the journal is based on its bibliometrics. Be aware, however, that the journal's Scopus status will say little about the "academic perception" of the journal, which depends on whether the academic community sees it as a solid or a well-respected journal or not.

In 2017 Mortality's impact factor was 0.270, which made it:

o   Q2 (second quartile) in philosophy
o   Q3 (third quartile) in health (social sciences)
o   Q1 (first quartile) in religious studies

This means that the IF of Mortality in 2017 would make it a top journal in religious studies, a decent journal in philosophy but a relatively low-ranking journal in health (social sciences, which is a separate field from medicine). The reason behind these different performances is that, perhaps more important than what your impact factor is, is the IF of competing journals in your field. When your journal is indexed in Scopus it will be allocated to one or more fields (sociology, medicine, biology) and be ranked in all of these disciplines.

So, 0.270 is enough to hit the top quartile of religious studies, which is a "slow field" and has only 3 journals with an IF higher than 1. But 0.270 is a relatively low IF in health (social sciences) that includes some highly quantitative journals. Indeed, taking into account that the first 32 journals have an IF over 1, 0.270 is enough only to hit Q3. In philosophy, the first 33 ranked journals have an impact factor higher than one and this is due to the presence of psychology journals (a relatively fast field) also classified as philosophy journals. But after the journal ranked no. 33, the IF of other journals sharply decreases, making it possible to hit Q2 with an IF of 0.270.

How to distinguish a 'good' conference from a 'bad' conference?

There are many ways to tell a good from a bad conference. My personal definition of a good conference is one where you get more than you invested. To go to a conference you invest time, money, perhaps have to prepare a presentation, socialize and spend long evenings at social dinners. Is it worth it?

I believe that you will bring home little if you just go to sessions. What would be the difference between watching the conference via streaming and being there? So, my general rule is that you have to work your way through each day during a conference: give and take business cards, speak to as many people as you want, drink as much beer as you can (possibly in the company of colleagues, rather than alone). A conference is a place where you socialize with colleagues and look for potential collaborators. My personal strategy, as I matured through the years, is to not spend lots of time at the panels, but at the exhibitions and social events. I sometimes attend panels, if friends are presenting or I need to meet someone in person and I know they are presenting there, but I always get the most from a conference in the socializing spaces. There, you can see the latest books, talk to colleagues, publishers and any other attendants. In the end, your success in networking greatly depends on how people see you as a person. Do they think you are fun, interesting or they can get something from you?

I recently undusted my guitar skills, after many years of a musical hibernation and a friend, hearing that, found a guitar for me in a cold Dnepro night, during an international conference. We spent most of the night at a local pub swapping the instrument between us to share our music with two friends. Many other colleagues were present and had fun. It was a long night, we got free drinks and my memories are a bit vague but the next days I could see the sympathetic looks on my colleagues' faces. We were the ones in charge of fun and many of them had appreciated it. Scientists are also people and, inasmuch as they like to discuss business, they also want to have fun, from time to time. In the end, I think that night was more important for networking than any other activity I could have joined at that conference.

But how can you know in advance that it is worth going to a given event? Or at least on what criteria can you get an estimation to know how likely it is that you will go home happy. There is nothing more frustrating than investing time and money to then go home and think "I'd have been better off staying at home, this trip was not worth my time."

There is no answer to this question as it depends on your own priorities at a given moment. Sometimes you just need to deliver a presentation at a large conference to please the donor or your university; some other times you know that some colleagues, whom you enjoy working with, are going. Sometimes it is worth it to meet people working in a given university, or country. In some other cases, you know that you will have a chance to publish your work, in other ones you can present your published work.

There are interdisciplinary conferences, regional conferences (gathering anyone doing empirical research on a given geographical area) and policy conferences. In the beginning, perhaps, the best strategy is to attend a few and see where you feel more comfortable, where you are appreciated most, where you feel that you can do without. Eventually, the choice of a conference or another also determines where (geographically, and disciplinary speaking) you feel you will have more chances to develop your career. At the European Anthropology Association, you will not meet (so many) political scientists, nor many American scholars. You can thus do your networking exercise with a given category of people from a given region of the world.

In the beginning of my career, I tended to concentrate on international workshops. A conference is a larger investment in terms of time and, possibly, money that I did not want to (or simply could not) spend, not always at least. Workshops were cheaper, there was more interaction with participants and I had more chances to interact with people more senior than I was, to see how they received me. I am still reluctant to go to large conferences but now I have many friends who sometimes attend, and I know I can at least meet with them. Would this strategy work for everyone, I do not know? In the end, it is about finding a niche for yourself, but that comes slowly, as everything else, in academia.

Being an assessor, evaluator or reviewer is time-consuming: why to bother?

What are the perks of becoming an evaluator or assessor for projects? Some people might see it as an extra income opportunity and in some cases, it is true. You are paid extra. But the cost-benefit analysis is "not the same" for everyone. It basically depends on how fast you are at reading, digesting, commenting. I know people who need 1-2 days to do a peer review for a journal. They still do reviews, but then they lose almost half of the working week to give comments to someone they do not know and, in general, do something they cannot claim any credit for. The same can be said for assessing books or projects. You are often paid but if you are a slow reader, or meticulous thinker, the money is not enough to buy out the time you lose. You ultimately know how fast you read, think and assess so you know how to decide how much you can take on. But in a long-term perspective, evaluations and assessments are an investment in your career.

Peer reviews of articles

There is somehow an expectation that you need to perform a given number of peer reviews per year. They are not formally required but you will be looked at like an alien if you declare that you have never done one, or one for a good journal. There is also a tacit reciprocity expectation: if you want your articles to be reviewed (and get people to spend time thinking of constructive comments for you), you should do the same for other, anonymous, scholars.

Besides, a top journal contacting you to perform a review may be regarded as evidence of the fact that you are visible or sufficiently established in your field to be contacted as an expert on a topic, or area.

Sometimes a peer review is also a way to see where research in your area is going, learn about a paper on similar topics submitted. In addition, by spotting mistakes and imperfections, and in general by looking critically at someone's work, might help you to better identify your own mistakes or understand what are the (potential) weakest points of an article.

Because it is unpaid, a peer review is, in some respects, a favor that you do for a journal. Once you submit an article to that very journal the editor might know your name. At any rate, you lose anonymity and you could simply mention that you reviewed for them when contacting one of the editors to discuss a possible submission and if the topic is suitable. Sometimes this could end up a win by you being invited to be on the editorial board (for instance if you have done many reviews and the journal is happy with your work).

Peer reviews of book proposals

Similar considerations apply to peer review of books: it is a sign that you are becoming established and a contact point with a series editor (sometimes, if the process is managed by an academic; there are cases where you are just in touch with an editorial assistant). The main difference is that you are paid some token that might be worth the effort, or not, depending on how fast you are able to write a review.

Peer reviews of funding applications

This is a much more a complex market and a proposal evaluator might become a full-time job. But, to become an evaluator for jobs that are paying well, you need to show previous experience in evaluation. You might thus want to start from the bottom, that is from donors that offer little or no money just to later claim that you are an experienced evaluator.

From a more strategic perspective, you will have a chance to see how projects are evaluated and, once you want to submit your own proposals, you will know more than a newcomer. You can also see how, and what, other people write, what are the most common mistakes in a project, thus becoming more skilled in spotting your own possible shortcomings.

In some cases, you might be given projects in your area, or topic, so to better understand what the tendencies are. Of course, it is illegal—or at least considered a conflict of interest—to submit your own project to a foundation for which you are doing evaluations for at the same time. But you could still assess one year and submit the next one, when you will be more knowledgeable, or more inspired.

Shining:
Stand out, getting visible, fame in academia

| How can I know if I am considered a good scholar? |

I was invited, or better, I got myself invited to teach in a summer school program. The organizers, a brilliant group of PhD students from the Baltics, shared with me a dilemma they faced within the organization.

They had received funding to hold a summer school session on "The Anthropology of Peace" and they had found a few speakers, but they were still lacking a keynote speaker. They wanted a good one but on what basis could they distinguish a "good" one from a "bad" one?

If you have been in the academic sector for some years, you probably have a good idea of what criteria you want your keynote speaker to fulfill. However, they were young, enthusiastic and clueless so decided to ask some of their professors for advice.

As often as not, to get a good answer you need to formulate your question in a proper and clear way. They went for, "If you had to name the Michael Jackson of the field, whom would that be?"

Apart from being an excellent question, this formulation unveils the lack of universal standards to talk about colleagues. There are two possible starting points to elaborate on criteria to be used to assess an academic.

The first suggests that you are a good academic inasmuch as other academics think highly of you, appreciate you and are willing to recommend you as a person and your work. This is an incredibly subjective criterion and keeps into account not only the quality of your work but also the reputation of integrity, and collegiality, that you have earned amongst your peers.

Colleagues who know you might look at whether, or how often, you have stolen someone's ideas, how you treat your PhD students, how constructive you are in your criticisms. They also see how available you are to give feedback or how available you are to help other people. This, obviously, in addition to what they think of your work. In many respects, however, it becomes difficult to endorse, or express admiration for, a colleague whose works are well known in the field, but who is also notorious for stealing ideas, patronizing or mobbing colleagues and students and being difficult to work with. At least, I would find it difficult to either work, or suggest someone to work, with such individuals.

This is to say that the academic community has its own approach. When talking about someone, their impact factors, h-index, citations and other quantitative criteria may sometimes be at the center of a conversation. I have heard colleagues amazed by the number of books, or citations, some other colleagues have. However, you will rarely hear "that scholar is great or good because they have over 10000 citations," or "because they published ten books in the past ten years." Metrics could be used to reinforce a statement, for instance "that scholar does very interesting stuff and is extremely productive," or "that person produces excellent studies and in addition, their works are highly cited." But citations alone do not justify authority. I can easily imagine a case of someone who has thousands of citations, but they are not taken seriously anyway (e.g., "Yes, that scholar is highly cited, but I cannot understand why; their writing is nothing special."). Academics still often use a criterion that is highly unmeasurable, intangible and volatile: reputation.

By contrast, the opposite standpoint is easier to measure and its objective. Or better, it has a claim of objectivity that stems from a public administration approach. In an ideal world, public administration endorses a high standard of transparency and criteria to the point that human agency is almost annihilated. In other words, the main claim of a public administration is that any of its workers, in that given function and before that given choice, would make the same decision. In an attempt to translate positivism into the art of ruling a country, bureaucracy refers to figures, and elements that are allegedly objectively measurable, to make sure everyone is treated the same way.

In theory, this is extremely meritocratic and democratic. You show better results and you are considered more important than someone with worse results. But in academia you cannot just measure numbers. I appreciate the position in which politicians and bureaucrats are. They need to find a way to make sense of the growing number of universities, scholars, academic productions, who are under pressure to show that public money is well spent. They might have to explain to the taxpayers where their money went. And they cannot say, "Thanks to your money one of our universities published a well-respected paper." What is well respected? What is good?

This means that the primary question asked by a ministry, or a quality control institution, is not "how good," but "how many?" In other words, there is a growing consensus on the use of quantitative indicators to measure quality. Quality control is often outsourced to the corporate sector. Databases are created and scholars are called upon to check the quality of journals, to ensure that they run a fair and professional peer review process. But then the journals are ranked according to their impact factor, which depends on how many times their documents have been cited by other journals. In practice, to tell a better journal from a less good one, it seems sufficient to look at their metrics.

As it is built, the system looks out for certain quality standards. However, in an effort to objectivize quality criteria, and make them understandable to everyone, the process through which academic reputation is constructed for public administration institutions has been drained by a number of standards, values and references that the academic community still regards as important. The question becomes, therefore, whom do you want to consider you a good scholar? The academic community, or the institutions in charge of quality control in your country?

These two do not necessarily overlap and I can easily imagine a situation in which your line manager says, "I believe you are an excellent scholar, and I like your work a lot, your logic and your research points to very interesting conclusions. However, according to the indicators that we have received from our ministry, you are under-performing. You are publishing in the wrong format, in the wrong outlets and these are not taken into account in our national assessment exercise...you are fired!"

It is your job to identify and target the right outlets. But there might be cases where, in spite of being widely appreciated by the academic community, you are the black sheep of your department. This is because you do not contribute enough to meeting their research output targets.

How democratic should policy decisions be on science?

De-elitization of universities means that a government needs to be able to explain, to large audiences, how taxpayer's money is spent. Citizens have, at least in theory, the right to vote. We are not at the Eurovision song level, where you can cast your vote in real time, but public accountability requires that institutions, while fulfilling their missions, maintain the trust of the people they are funded by (taxpayers, so virtually anyone in a country).

People should be able to choose where their money goes and contribute to the policies and politics of the country they live in. This is the very sense of democracy. However, and this is a question that goes much further than academia, how much power should be left to people who contribute to decisions on topics that they do not necessarily understand?

My job is to read and think, I have spent years "domesticating myself" into the scientific community and trying to understand what my peers and colleagues write about. And I do not always manage to understand everything. So, what is the percentage of a population of a country that, asked whether to fund this or that research, will have sufficient knowledge to make a conscious and informed choice? Some years ago, the governor of Florida suggested to cut funding for anthropological programs across the state because they did not lead to the production of real jobs.[5]

The prompt, and smart, answer by a large community of anthropology graduates demonstrated that anthropology produced excellent workers. But these workers did not flow en masse into a single career. They had learned to work with people and applied their new skills to a variety of contexts. So yes, there was no direct link between graduating in anthropology and getting a given job. But anthropology offered a number of intangible skills that would eventually benefit the society and the job market.

In their excellent book, and blog, and now mediatic phenomenon *Freakonomics*,[6] Stephen Dubner and Steven Levitt share another anecdote, incidentally also related to Florida. They were consulted by the local administration on the possibility to liquidate all pedestrian crossings in a given town. The rationale was simple: statistically, the great majority of

---

[5]   See the debate at: http://blogs.plos.org/neuroanthropology/2011/10/11/florida-govern or-anthropology-not-needed-here/

[6]   http://freakonomics.com/

accidents resulting in death or harm to pedestrians happened while crossing a pedestrian crossing. By eliminating them, thus, the local administration expected to drastically reduce the amount of accidents in that town.

As the authors of the blog explained, the majority of accidents happen there because this is where people are supposed to be. More people die per square kilometer where a hospital is located because this is where sick people go. From a statistics standpoint, by liquidating hospitals, we can also get rid of those places where average mortality is higher than in the rest of the country. But do we really need to get rid of hospitals?

Without second-guessing, the reasonings proposed to eliminate anthropology or pedestrian crossings make sense and sound appealing. It is sufficient to claim, "Our goal is to reduce accidents," or "Our goal is to link a university to the job market so that your children can find a job easily once they graduate." Emotionally, I would be inclined to believe these statements. However, after reflecting on the indirect effects of this decision, I might conclude that it is not the best idea ever.

Academics, the scientific community, but also a number of experts are paid to (allegedly) think. Not only to think but to reflect on medium and long-term consequences of a given decision, to spend time considering a variety of options and possibly inform decision makers on available alternatives and solutions. Leaving the decisions in the hands of an academic, or an expert, the community means to exclude most of a society from some of the decision-making processes. Giving an equal vote to all the individuals of a society might mean to leave a significant amount of decision power in the hands of those who might not have the time to reflect on the broader effects of a given decision, possible alternatives, or its long-term consequences.

What I need to do vs. what I want to do: is there a balance for an academic career?

The above reflections on academic goals might sound deceiving. How can I enjoy my job when I have to work in two different directions? One to satisfy the academic community and one to satisfy my quality control institutions? This might get even more complicated if what you really love to do does not sufficiently overlap with neither of the above. If you are in academia, I would assume that peer acceptance, respect and in general your own reputation

119

are important to you. In some cases, you might want to boost your competitive spirit and find satisfaction in fulfilling the criteria required by your ministry or national control institution or feel that you have a respectful place in your institutions (i.e., that the managing board and the administration admire you).

But we are not robots. At some stage in your career, you might want to develop some skills that are not necessarily required in your field or sector. You might fall short of motivation to perform certain tasks or you might want to try new things. There are a number of academics that change career paths, or sectors, in the course of their professional life but many stay and just find their niche.

An administration might want to put too much pressure on you and push you into doing certain tasks and taking directions that you do not like. Think of the growing demand for academics that are able to find external funding for projects and to manage projects. What if you are a bad manager or simply not motivated to be a manager? In principle, when you made the choice to work as a scientist you committed to a career of research and teaching but knew little about the administrative tasks you had to face.

Any research institution, just like any other working unit, is made of a team. There is a clear profile to become part of the team, but this is just the ideal profile. In reality, the success of a team depends also on its diversity. It pays little to have all ten people with the same characteristics and it is possibly more useful to have people sufficiently different to be able to perform a diversity of tasks depending on what is demanded at a given moment. Think of a football team. You might want all of your players to be fit, tall, fast, with good ball control, good nerves and a vision. That would be the most ideal team ever. Instead, you will get a very good player who is not tall enough but runs so fast that they are perfect for a specific role. Someone who is slower but so tall is always needed when having to catch a flying ball. Then the most talented player has little nerves and sometimes gets very hot-headed. And then a short player, even a bit fat, not too fast. But that player is a sort of genius and you take them as he is.[7] The question here is not, "Why does not everyone fit the criteria of the perfect player," but "Can I live

---

[7]   If you were born before 1980, we are thinking of the same person.

with that," or "Do all these players fit well together?" If yes, then there is no need to change anything.

By the same token, in a research team, you do not need that 100% of your researchers are great fundraisers. If you have enough of them to meet your target, the others do not need to concentrate on fundraising. Perhaps your best fundraiser is not a devoted teacher and you might want to liberate them from these tasks to spend more time on a funding application. In contrast, one of the "bad" fundraisers loves teaching and perhaps they can take on some extra courses. This will require them to teach more but they know that you will turn a blind eye on their limited fundraising skills.

There are several ways to pull together a research team, depending on what you need. One of your members could be a media catalyst who will always be on TV, capable to explain to large audiences what your laboratory, or research group, is doing. They might not be the best researcher ever but, as long as you need publicity, you need that very person in your team.

Some scientists have a reputation because they write highly cited articles. Some others are famous because are always on TV. They do not write much anymore but everybody in the country knows them and they bring visibility and publicity. Some others might be recognized for other characteristics.

So, I would construct my profile, or find my niche, in a hypothetical department, based on the following:

1. you need to survive—if someone is paying your salary, you need to do at least the minimum to deserve this salary. If this means to deliver a number of outputs, you need to do it (or change your job, if that's impossible)

2. you need to be happy—if you devote yourself to 8 or more hours per day to something, you need to at least be content, if not happy. Especially in academia, few are here for the money. Academics are usually over-educated. It should thus not be too difficult to requalify, change careers, and get yourself a job that you hate but earns you lots of money.

In the end, it is important, at least to me, that you:

- o Do what you want, what you like, and what makes you feel alive.
- o Are sufficiently motivated to do what you do—I am not talking about annoyances and small boring tasks that will always be there, no matter how interesting your job is.
- o Do what you need to do to not be fired. There is a bottom line and going under it will get you in trouble. It would be safer to stay a bit above that line and more rewarding to be able to deliver enough to win the esteem of your boss and colleagues. If you are not interested in this, at least do what you need to do to be considered an active researcher.
- o Find a compromise with your boss. There might be some other colleagues who can offer other skills better than you can. But you do have a specialty, things for which you are appreciated for and, eventually, are an added value to the department. Think and discuss with your bosses what are your unique contributions and how you can make up for other people who are less performative than you in some tasks. If you do this, it will be easier not to feel pressure for other things that you are unhappy to do or that are just not very good at.
- o Find a compromise with the academic world and what you can offer. An ideal research career consists of a number of steps that not everybody can do, not at the same pace at least. For one thing, everybody wants an article in the top journal of their discipline but not everyone will get there. What are the strong points that you can offer your peers so as to enhance your reputation and get appreciated? That could be as simple as being someone who is fun when explaining things. You could be the "humorous academic" in your entourage. You will probably never get a Nobel prize, but your colleagues will know when to look for you and appreciate you.

Frustrations and survival

No matter how good you are, there will always be reasons to get frustrated. If you had 15 articles last year, your expectations might be that you have 17 this year and go on growing forever. If last year you picked 500, 1000, 2000 citations, you might (reasonably) expect that this year you will pick more since you are more famous, have more articles or are advertising more. But where is the limit? And what happens if you do not publish the 17 articles you had as a target but "only" 14?

In principle, I embrace the idea that life, and in particular professional life, is a crescendo of successes. That is that, apart from some sporadic cases (i.e., when you win a Nobel prize, then you can only go down, or when you are discredited for some reason), chances to get better rewarded increase as you get more experienced.

However, getting more rewarded, or getting more satisfaction, also depends on how you measure things, what are your values and against what criteria you assess your success.[8]

You can publish a book per year but then a colleague, who publishes only one in five years, gets a contract with Oxford University Press, a place where you would never dare to go. You have more citations than someone else in the past three years but overall, they have more than you have. And you get frustrated. Or vice versa, you end up envying someone who has been advancing faster than you in the past three or four years. Someone else publishes much less than you but they are always in the media, and thus much more visible than you are. Maybe someone is much more productive than you, but you know they have no children, or they have but they are already grown up, so they spend more time working than you do.

We are different and there are a hundred more reasons to get frustrated. There are only a few chances that you can consider yourself satisfied according to some hypothetical universal criteria. There will always be criteria that you do not meet. But you can still consider yourself happy and satisfied with what you have and by your own criteria. It all depends on your life values. Sometimes it is good to stop and reflect not only about what you have achieved professionally but in your life in general. Perhaps you have achieved less than that colleague of yours but have also invested less in your work. By contrast, you have devoted most of your weekends to your family, children or hanging around with friends. Or you have developed some other

---

[8]   Other brilliant suggestions can be found in "The Subtle Art of Not Giving a F*ck" by Mark Manson https://markmanson.net/books/subtle-art

skills, practiced hobbies or simply like to watch movies, take walks in the woods, swim or do other things and you are in good physical shape.

(Lack of) career and personal development: somehow a success story

A friend and colleague of mine for many years had to face several decisions that somehow limited his career. He started as a researcher at a relatively young age and with good perspectives to progress to associate and then perhaps full professor. However, 15 years after his entry into the tenure track system, he is still formally a junior academic.

In the course of the past fifteen years, he had to face a number of choices, most of which related to his family life, that made it difficult for him to concentrate on his career. He had to travel a lot, basically living, and teaching, in two different places at the same time. Most of the formal criteria he had to meet to keep his job were related to teaching, thus leading him to neglect the research aspect of his work.

At a given stage, because of personal issues, he had to give up one teaching position and remain in the other. He eventually got stuck in his junior position in the other university because he was too busy with other things to take care of strategic elements for his career.

This might not sound like a success story and I agree that, professionally, it could have gone better. However, the point here is not to look at the professional development in itself but within a context.

During a recent conversation, he said, "I know my line manager might think that I wasted my talent, and energy, because of my choice of dividing my life like I did so far, but that gave me other chances. I learned a language and about a culture, and this is important not only for me personally but also professionally. As a scientist, in fact, I am a bridge between two languages and two cultures, a thing that I believe is very important in my field."

> In addition, I would add that he lives in a small but beautiful house a five minutes' walk from the beach, has been contributing to the education of two splendid children and plays in a music band. He might not be the most organized and career-oriented person I know but, to the best of my knowledge, he has little understanding of the word "stress."
>
> Now, I am not sure this would work for me or for many other people but, to a certain extent, it worked for him. He is not the most famous scholar, but he has his friends and admirers and also contributes to research projects. He is not the most active and cited scholar in the field, but neither is he doing much about it nor is he getting frustrated. So, all in all, if looked at from my perspective, I see this as a success story.

This does not mean that any personal successes can make up for the fact that you do not deliver. One thing is to have the minimal required output. A different thing is to under-perform. Mostly this depends on your energy and motivation to do things, which vary during the course of life. A book with Yale University Press will look impressive on your CV, but make sure that, by engaging in this project, you do not fail to deliver other outputs that are required by your national evaluation system. By the same token, community services such as evaluations, peer reviews and committees take time and energy, up to the point of not leaving you enough time to perform your standard (and expected) duties.

Your career choices are yours, the bottom line is to be able to make choices that allow you to perform at least above the threshold between an active researcher (that is, a researcher considered having a positive impact according to national evaluation criteria) and a non-active one. Once you do this, you can decide whether to invest in further activities that are fully recognized by your ministry, or into something else. But if you do not do enough, your position will be at risk and this might eventually affect your personal life as well.

The risks of metrics

The increased popularity of databases, maintained by commercial publishers, and the identification of bibliometric criteria to assess science has served the scope of making things more "measurable." You might not necessarily agree with the way they are measured, but a great majority of academic assessments take advantage of them. In the end, either you create your own assessment methods, and lobby for it, or need to put up with what you are requested to do. This does not necessarily mean to blindly do whatever you are requested to do. It is rather about making your employer happy. With the rest of your efforts invested in things you believe in but that are not necessarily acknowledged as "useful" by your bureaucracy.

In other words, bibliometric measurements, databases and a number of other criteria are important, across countries, regions and disciplines. They are sometimes used during quality control exercises and for national rankings but also at an individual level (when assessing candidates who applied for a scholarship or other government-paid positions).

Bibliometric criteria are not only easier to evaluate because you can just draw the statistics from a database. They are cheap to use because they can be calculated mechanically. Finally, they bear in themselves a claim of objectivity because they are based on figures, and conventional wisdom suggests that once you have numbers, there is little to explain. Numbers are objective, but the choice of some indicators instead of others, or of the algorithm used to generate these numbers, is a subjective one.

Case study—the list of the best academic publishers in Estonia

Estonia has spent a great deal of effort to come up with a system enabling universities, and public institutions, to rank academic outputs, academics and their departments. But they have also faced a challenge. On the one hand, it was necessary to find a way to make Estonian research measurable against international standards. On the other one, however, Estonia was still a low performing country when measurement standards were conceived. As a result, the system had to find a balance between ambitions, expectations and reality so to measure academic output against realistic criteria.

To give you an example of unrealistic criteria, think of the case where, almost overnight, only Scopus publications came to count towards tenure or to apply for research money. Scopus publications are, on average, harder to get than general "academic publications," of which there is no universally agreed academic standard. If you have a choice between Scopus and non-Scopus journals, I would assume that a substantial number of scientists would choose a shortcut and go for a non-Scopus scientific publication. When the bar is raised, and only Scopus publications are counted, a large majority of scholars find themselves lagging behind. Putting pressure on people might be a way to produce change but it will also be met with resistance by some. For instance, think of the "old guard," that is established scholars who occupy relevant positions and advise the government, have built their career, prestige and reputation on different values. Endorsing the new criteria means, for them, not only to admit that they did not produce enough quality but also to "disqualify" themselves for some tasks or activities (i.e., not qualify anymore for the formal requirements to consult governments or to apply for some research grants).

In other words, there might be situations where the great majority of your scientists are not used to publishing internationally, and some others actively oppose change in measurement standards. If you create rules only prizing international publications your country will undergo a "transition phase" (that could last for years) during which the majority, or a large fraction, of your scientists do not meet the minimal quality requirements set. This is a bit like shooting yourself in the foot. If you want people to adopt certain standards, these standards need to be realistic and you need to provide some support to those willing to grow to meet them.

One of the compromises Estonia has come up with is a classification of "best academic publishers" that is relatively flexible. Keep in mind that there is no Scopus-equivalent database for books. It is easy to imagine that Harvard University Press is a top one but what about Liverpool University Press? Should it be considered "good" or "not so good" by quality-control authorities? And Edinburgh University Press? They both have good reputations among scholars, but "reputation" is not tangible or justifiable through formal criteria.

Besides, because publishing a book is less of an achievement in science than in the social sciences there is not much urgency in the creation of such a database. Still, countries need to be able to classify academic publishers, and therefore authors, somehow. In some countries, the ministry makes an inquiry among universities that have to provide a list of the publishers that they consider of the highest quality. The result is a list of double standards. The best publishers are there but also publishers where employees from each university have published in. What would you do if someone came to you and asked what are the best publishers in the world and you knew that, based on this classification, your university (or department) might be praised as the best in the country or be scorned as an unproductive one? It would be fair to assume that your list of best publishers would include the best-known ones and the ones where your staff publishes (otherwise you admit that your staff willingly targets low-quality publishers).

Your argument would then be: yes, Harvard is better, but this or that publisher also have excellent quality, and this is why we publish there. On the other side of the spectrum, we have the classification used by some countries that, in a quest for top excellence, give credit to books only with the top academic publishers in the world. For example, the list of A+ publishers in Hong Kong includes no more than 17 publishers. Anything else is considered of lower standard.

Estonia is somehow halfway between them. The list of best academic publishers includes books by publishers that have more than 500 titles in 5 major European libraries selected by the ministry of research. It makes sense. If main libraries keep on buying books from that publisher, and they are respectable libraries, then the publisher must be good.

If you have many titles from the same publisher, it means that the public, and scholars in particular, appreciate that publisher. A conclusion may be that the publisher in question is good and prints good quality books.

This is a good assumption but not necessarily accurate. To have 500 titles in a library, a publisher needs to publish 500 or possibly more books. Only large academic publishers can meet this criterion. Think of independent publishers that produce only a few titles per year, carefully check their product, quality and look meticulously over details that commercial publishers leave behind focusing more on quantity than quality. To publish 500 or more books will take them years, let alone to have 500 titles in major libraries. In a similar fashion, think of open-access e-publishers. If they do not sell your books, it is likely that libraries will not buy them and you remain out of the list.

As a scholar, you may have to work like a dog to be able to publish with that publisher, go through several peer reviews and other painful tasks but, as long as national rankings are concerned, you will get no credit. And then, when your job is on the line, this could be a deciding factor and your university might ask you why you did not go for a more standard publisher. Or your administration might reason this way "Yes, it is a good book, but it is not a top publisher. We trust companies that have published many books. In fact, figures show that they issue first class books."

This also means that books by publishers that are "sausage factories" will be there by force of numbers. It is sufficient that someone sees a sexy title, thinks that the book will be relevant for their research and orders it. If a publisher issues 500 books per year, in ten years they get 5000 titles published. It is then sufficient that 10% of their books are purchased for the publisher to be admitted into the Olympus (or the hall of fame, for those unacquainted with Greek Mythology) of best publishers.

A commercial publisher is interested in increasing their profits more than producing quality books. The more they publish, the more they sell, the more they make. Incidentally, the more they sell, the more they are likely to have 500 titles in a library and thus be considered a first-class publisher. This is not the only approach that has flaws. In reality, any system that tries to set general rules for a large population will fail to take into account some situations, or case-limits, and turn out to be too inclusive or too exclusive.

Here is the list of publishers, for those who want to check it. What may catch your eye is the pacific co-existence of top publishers with mid-range and even low range ones. For the ministry they all count as 2.1 (a book with a top publisher) but, all the rest are equal, why bother going with

Harvard University Press when you can shoot much lower and get the same amount of credits from and for your institution?[9]

There are two conclusions that I would suggest:

First, academics in the country may be divided into two categories: those who publish with the best publishers and those who publish with companies that, although not of high-quality, satisfy the ministry's criteria for high-quality output. In theory, in the eye of a public institution, they are worth more or less the same so, unless you have a real motive to go with a top publisher, you can easily live with a low profile one.

Second, there is a thin line between those interested in publishing with the most prestigious publishers and those who prefer to go with lower level publishers but still get credit for it. If the formal credits you will get for either of the publishers is the same, only a fraction of the scientists in the country will prioritize top publishers. They will earn a better reputation but the same amount of credits than those publishing with lower level publishers. The rest will be more concerned with survival. In other words, both categories can have their cake and eat it too. But in the former case, they can add some whipped cream or a cherry on it. How much are you ready to work for that cherry and whipped cream?

How to publish in a Scopus journal?

In theory, there is no formal difference between getting an article published into an academic journal and an academic journal that is indexed in Scopus (or WoS). That is, the only merit these journals have, with regards to non-Scopus ones is that they applied for, and were admitted into, a database that is widely considered as a standard for academic excellence.

The journal underwent a formal evaluation and it was deemed worth inclusion into a database. The quality of articles may vary a bit across issues, just as editing and peer reviews will depend on the subjective judgment of the editorial team and of the reviewers, although some widely accepted standards are applied.

---

[9]   See the complete list at https://www.etis.ee/Portal/Classifiers/Index?lang=ENG

The main difference between a good journal and a not so good one in academia is, however, (surprise yourself) human agency. Any academic journal of a decent level is supposed to have an editorial board, one or more editors and have an embedded peer review process for all articles. However, there is considerable variation in quality across journals depending on:

Quality standards of the editor in chief and the editorial board: scholars are different; they have different approaches and standards. Someone who is used to certain quality standards might ignore some criteria that for other people are important. In addition, not all editors are equally motivated to do their job. Some might just be there by chance, because they need that position or because they were asked. Devotion to the cause is, therefore, also, important.

Interaction of the editorial board: in some journals, members of the editorial board barely know that they are part of the board (sometimes they are there because their name looks good on paper). In some others, they meet regularly and make decisions. In some cases, we are talking about scholars with lots of excellent connections, who know established scholars, who are motivated and who have good quality standards themselves. In other cases, they might not be motivated or have sufficient experience or connections, or simply do not interpret their role actively enough.

Articles turnover: the priority of a journal is to regularly publish issues according to a pre-defined plan. Having many articles makes it more likely to receive good quality ones. But receiving only a few submissions per year leads you to a dilemma: to publish whatever we have on hand when the journal needs to go to print or to skip the issue. Neither option is good for the journal's reputation so, all in all, journals with a higher article turnover are more likely to publish better articles.

Peer review process: journals have different standards. In some cases, they send the article to only one reviewer whereas in some other cases they might solicit feedback from four or five more academics. In some cases, one round of reviews is sufficient. In some other cases, the article might undergo two or even three rounds of reviews before being accepted. Fifteen reviewers and eight peer review rounds do not necessarily guarantee quality (but definitely guarantee a significant waste of time) but, on average, the more accurate the peer review process, the more likely the article will have better quality standards.

131

Reviewers: anyone active in research can act as a reviewer. But reviewers may have different quality standards, preferences and tastes. When an editor looks for reviewers for a given article, they could stop at the first person with some expertise on the topic of the article or require more specific criteria. You might want a reviewer that is recognized in the field, or someone who is known for reviewing quickly and on time, or for being constructive and providing good advice. You might also want, in some cases, a very critical reviewer or a tough one. You definitely do not want someone providing destructive criticism or taking a year to review an article. But this happens, especially when you do not know your reviewers or do not search for them accurately. Some journals handpick their reviewers and keep an internal database of good ones and not so good ones. The better you handle the review process, the more likely you are to receive articles from established academics (possibly delivering good quality articles, even if this is not guaranteed) who want to avoid wasting time and nerves on a submission.

The better a journal deals with the above points, the more likely it is to deliver quality, the more it becomes likely to receive good articles and to keep good quality throughout time. In some cases, this may lead the journal to improve its reputation and getting ranked higher in Scopus. However, this is not automatic, and this is possibly an idiosyncrasy of the system. Ranking in Scopus (and WoS) is based on the impact factor of a journal, calculated as the number of citations vs. published documents over a given period. This is based on the perception that good articles are widely read and cited, keeping the journal up in the rankings. However, it might also go the other way around and an article might by default be considered good because it is in a given journal that already has a good reputation. It might also mean that low-quality articles, if widely cited, bring a journal up in the rankings and good quality articles that remain unnoticed (and uncited) sink the journal in the rankings.

In general, I think it is fair to assume that better-ranked journals can be considered better journals, but the association is not automatic. I have seen excellent journals who remain low in rankings for several reasons. They publish on a very specific topic that is of interest to few academics. Or else their editors do not invest enough in the citation rush (some journals invest a lot of efforts to get the highest number of citations every year). In the end, one might ask the question: Which came first, the chicken or the egg? Some journals receive more, and better, articles because they are higher in rankings or are they higher in rankings because they are perceived as good and scholars with better articles tend to submit to them?

At any rate, the evaluation system in most countries leads you to assume that a journal ranked Q1 in Scopus is better than a Q2 (or lower) one. In some cases, you will get more credits if you publish in a Q1 journal. As a result, scholars might submit to a Q1 journal because they want more benefits from an article, not necessarily because they think that the journal is better than another ranked Q2 or Q3. Or they might assume that a journal in Q1 is better, leading that journal to receive many more submissions than others that are, sometimes, better suited or better managed.

If you are targeting a Scopus journal, your focus depends on two things: what you want to do and what you need to do. As an academic looking for glory and fame (do they exist in academia?) you need to target a Q1 journal, which is allegedly read by more people than a Q2, Q3 or Q4. However, you are not the only one thinking like this so Q1 journals are the most "crowded" ones. They possibly receive more manuscripts, have slower turnaround times, harder review processes and a number of other barriers.

Harder journals might be worth making the effort, but they are also a risk in that the publication of your manuscript might be delayed, or likelihood of rejection is higher. I once received a request to publish an article that had already been accepted by another (and "better") journal. The problem was that the article had to be printed before the end of the year to be considered for the national evaluation exercise, or the author might lose his job. I was incidentally short of an article at that time, so I sent it for review to colleagues whom I knew would review it quickly. Eventually, the article was accepted and published quickly (quickly in academia does not have the same meaning it has in real life). The author had to "downgrade" his publication from a Q1 to a Q3 journal, but he met his publication target for the assessment exercise.

There are journals that receive too many submissions and that allow themselves to reject your articles even if both reviewers suggest that the article is publishable after major revisions. But there are also many decent journals in Scopus that do not receive enough submissions and that would be happy to advise and guide you through the process eventually leading to publication with them. As in the case above, if you are required to publish in a Scopus journal (no matter which quartile) to keep your job, you might want to go for a lower ranked journal. Do what you are required to do and then concentrate on a better-ranked journal for the next article, when your job is not on the line anymore. It certainly pays to have articles in top journals, but they take more time and effort and the risk is that, if you have not published enough in a given period, you might be considered unproductive or inactive. This is why people often talk about a two-speed strategy in academia: one top journal every X years and lower ranked journals more often. The top journal represents quality and indicates that, when you want, you can write an excellent article. The lower ranked journals complement the picture by showing that you are active and productive all the time. In other words, you satisfy quality and quantity criteria altogether.

How do you enter Scopus (Web of Science or any other journal's hall of fame)?

We talk a lot about journals that are already in Scopus. But how did they end up there? Well, they applied, in the first instance. Requirements may change over time but, in general, you will need to show that your journal can maintain some quality standards, publishes regularly and it is read by an academic public.

Publishing regularly is easy. You just have to show that your journal comes out when it is supposed to. If you announce that you have an issue in June and in December, you should stick to these months. You can delay the issue by a few days but publishing the July issue in August is not really a safe thing to do.

Quality standards will be checked manually by some assessors who will read the last few issues of your journal. This process is done only once, when your journal is assessed. But I am not sure if it is repeated regularly once the journal has been admitted. I mean, there are obvious and tough obstacles to overcome before entering a database, but I doubt that articles are regularly checked after the journal enters the database. The general assumption is that, if quality decreases significantly, the database maintainers will get an alert and check the journal. By force of this, if quality decreases "a little bit," little or nothing will happen.

Finally, being read by an academic public means that other scholars engage with its articles by citing them. The usual assumption is that a fraction of those reading an article will cite it so, the more you are cited, the more you are read (allegedly). If your journal is evaluated positively under these criteria, you may be invited to join the database.

During the process, the impact factor (IF) of your journal will be calculated. If you have relatively few citations, your IF might even tend to be zero. In fact, the lowest ranking journals (in Q4) will have an IF close to zero. This is relatively unimportant in countries whose evaluation system tends to give credit to Scopus publications regardless of whether the journal is ranked first or last in its discipline. When this is the case, you simply need to publish in a Scopus-indexed journal but how high, or low, that journal is ranked is not important to your line manager, university or ministry. In such cases, it is up to you to decide how much extra you want to work. Let us say that publishing in a Q4 journal might take 3 months but a Q1 publication will take 6 or more months of writing. Are you ready to invest that much time or is a Q4 publication sufficient? Keep in mind that I am talking about general tendencies but there might be some Q4 journals that are just as hard to get in as Q1 ones.

Case study—non-English language journals and Scopus

Since 2011, I have co-edited a small independent and open access English language journal.[10] Some years ago, we applied to be included in Scopus and Web of Science (WoS).

We were requested to prove that the journal comes out regularly, in the agreed months, with no particular delays. We were also asked to submit the last few issues so that experts could go through the articles and assess their quality. Eventually, we were admitted into Scopus but not WoS.

The Scopus report mentioned that, although the articles of the journal were a bit under-cited, their quality was good enough to be allowed and

---

[10] Studies of Transition States and Societies (STSS) is entirely managed (and maintained) at Tallinn University. It was established in 2009 by a team led by my friend and colleague Raivo Vetik, to whom most of the credits for the initial achievements of the journal should go to and to whom I am very thankful for his brilliant initiative.

included in the database. WoS had the same reservation about the citations, but their decision was that we were not admitted in their database. What is important to notice, however, is that we were told in the WoS report that the number of citations we had was insufficient for admission into the database of a journal in English and with our disciplinary focus. In other words, citations for them were weighted against an internal standard.

I drew a few strategic lessons by reasoning on this distinction. I have no scientific evidence to back up my conclusions. But I am sharing them since it might be useful to keep them into account when making decisions about your journal. The Scopus database was established later than the WoS one, initially the main, and in some respects unique, one until some years ago. Indeed, institutions with a more conservative view on science assessment still refer to WoS as the one and only database. To be able to compete with WoS, Scopus had to position itself on the market and used a few approaches of which two are important to me. One is that Scopus attempted to become the largest (and thus most inclusive) existing database of scientific journals. The other is that Scopus has put a great deal of effort in the social sciences and humanities, which was not the initial focus of WoS. Scopus was thus more interested than WoS in our journal, and ready to bend a bit its quality criteria to include us. This allowed the database to continue its expansion and cover more a country that was under-represented so far.

There are now a few disagreements between scholars and assessment approaches. Some might say that Scopus is too inclusive and thus does not guarantee the quality of a journal. Some others say that WoS is too elitist, exclusive and leaves out excellent journals. Some evaluation systems will take into account articles published with either Scopus or WoS indexed journals but there is a shortcut. Most, not to say all, journals indexed in WoS are also indexed in Scopus but not all Scopus journals are indexed in WoS. So. This means that, if you do not know where you will apply for a job, the safest option is to publish in WoS journals since they are included in both databases. If you need to publish in a journal that is in any database then you can relax and pick a Scopus journal, since they are much more inclusive, and you have more to choose from.

At any rate, companies maintaining databases (i.e., Scopus, WoS) live as long as there is an interest for their database. They also grow inasmuch as they can expand to new countries that are interested in buying their product. Take a low research performance country, where few academics publish in Scopus-indexed journals and there are few, or even none, domestic journals indexed in Scopus. What would be the use of buying a service from Scopus if this allowed the country to assess only a fraction of the researchers working at local universities? This is to say that, to be able to sell its services to new countries, Scopus should be interested in admitting local journals into its database and make it easier for domestic researchers to be present in it. Only at that point can they sell an algorithm or a service allowing the ministry of education or research to evaluate their scholars through bibliometric criteria.

The way the assessment of our journal was formulated also suggested that the number of citations required to enter a database was weighed against the average number of citations that journals in the same discipline and same language have. Not only do some disciplines bring more citations than others (compare IF in astrophysics and anthropology journals) but, equally important, some languages bring more citations than others. English is the widely accepted language for science but, by far, not the only one. In fact, a scientific journal may exist in any language and, if it targets mostly the local scientific community, there is nothing against keeping it in a local language. After all Spanish, Russian, Chinese, French, and Arabic are widely spoken worldwide. By writing in one of these languages, you can still engage in debates with a number of countries. Accordingly, there are a number of non-English language journals both in Scopus and WoS.

In terms of citations, these journals cannot possibly reach the number of citations as an English language journal can. This makes me think that, had my journal been a non-English language one, would it have stood more chances to be admitted into the WoS. I am assuming here that the number of citations of a non-English language journal is lower than its

English counterparts. If the journal is in a language like Estonian and its citations are weighed against the average number of citations of other Estonian or Baltic language journals, then getting above the average in the region should be easy.[11]

This makes sense. If you do not use a pondering (weighing) system, you will never be able to admit journals that target a very small academic community and there is no reason why a journal cannot be in Latvian or in Georgian. They also have academic communities there, they do science and they have the right to publish in a language that allegedly everyone in the country speaks.

In terms of quality, inasmuch as admission into a database depends on quality, and quality needs to be checked by reading the articles published in your journal, journals published in different languages are assessed differently. Imagine that a journal in Maltese applies for Scopus. Who could assess the quality of these articles? I would guess only a Maltese speaker, a thing that cuts out most scientists in the world and reduces the pool of experts one can rely on for the job. Think also that the database might not have anyone who speaks the language available, so they would have to identify someone, who might be doing this kind of assessment for the first time.

My conclusion here is that different language journals might end up being assessed differently, and against quality criteria that vary a lot. This might also mean that, when establishing a new journal, it might make sense strategically to have it in a local language. A local language journal does not mean that you cannot publish in English. It simply means that the primary language of your journal is not English. For instance, you can have 2 issues per year in the local language and one in English or publish each issue in both languages.

---

[11] Estonia has a population of 1.4 million people. The academic community is only a fraction of the population and the Estonian speaking academic community is even smaller, given that Estonian universities have been very open in their recruitment policy and have hired a high number of foreign academics.

Why should I establish a journal in a language other than English?

I suggest above that establishing a journal in a local language might be a good approach. But some might object that the international scientific community widely uses English. Then why to remain at the margins of scientific debates by publishing, or managing a journal, in a local language?

First, English literacy varies across disciplines. Some national debates are still conducted in local languages. Second, it might be worth considering the level of access one might gain into public debates (schools, politics) by publishing in a local language, especially in countries where English is not widely known. Finally, you can still publish articles in both the local language and English. Some journals have, in fact, one or two issues in the local language and one or two in English throughout the year and may be considered local language journals.

At any rate, a journal in a local language offers the following advantages in my view:

Costs: English language editing is a cost and not a minor one. Even if you are a native English speaker, the time that you devote to reading all the articles to check the language is a cost, it is tiring and there is no guarantee that you will do a proper job. Copy editing is a job and there are people who specialize in this. Alternatively, you can ask the authors to be responsible for their own editing work, but there is no guarantee that they would do a proper job. It would be much easier for you to find someone for a final check in the local language of the journal and that would significantly cut costs.

Niche: in some countries, the number of good level journals is very low. Some countries have no journals at all indexed in Scopus in some disciplines. If well managed, your journal would rapidly occupy a niche at a national level and might become one of the forums where the national scientific community, or all scientists working in that language, debate some important issues.

Readership: there are millions of academic journals out there. Allegedly, each of them has ambitions to become well-read and a reference in a discipline or area of studies, where major scholars lust to publish. But how many of these succeed? English is the language in which there is the highest number of scientific journals, articles and documents. But you might want to try to stand out in the domestic market before going international. Perhaps, in the long term, you might also decide to stay and engage in national debates if they are sufficiently relevant in your country.

How to start an academic journal?

The initial ingredients to establish an academic journal are relatively basic. You need:

1. an editorial board to make decisions, identify reviewers, solicit articles
2. a managing team, to deal with the submission and processing of articles, layout, copy editing, and printing.

The problem, with a newfound academic journal, is starting up the engine to get it going. I am thinking of the gap in enthusiasm between those who have established the journal and potential authors. The editor in chief and the team will think, "We have just launched a new journal. Isn't it the most beautiful thing in the world? We have been working hard and are ready to offer the best service, fast peer reviews and lots of enthusiasm."

Potential authors will, at best, think, "Oh, there is another academic journal. The title sounds appealing. Now, let us see: if it does not discontinue after two issues, perhaps I will think of submitting something." Receiving articles is even more difficult because of "the Scopus economy." If my national evaluation system draws a line between Scopus articles and non-Scopus articles, to be able to claim credit for my work, I need to publish in Scopus journals. How can I, therefore, justify putting my efforts into an article that goes into a non-Scopus, and a just-born, journal?

I am here assuming that the new journal is not indexed in Scopus because, with few exceptions, it is unlikely that a newly established journal will be included from its very inception into the Scopus database. For one thing, it is impossible to check its quality because no articles have been published yet.

In principle, this means that virtually no scholar from a "Scopus country" (a country that gives credits to scientists if they publish in a Scopus, or another, database) will be tempted to submit an article. Here I see a great Catch-22: to receive good articles, you need to be indexed in Scopus; but to be indexed in Scopus, you have to demonstrate that you can publish good quality articles.

There is only one way out of this circle. You need to convince people, capable of writing good articles, that it is worth it to invest in your journal. True, your authors will not get their Scopus credit for publishing with you, but you can offer a few things:

o   A focus that no other existing journal is offering.
o   An editorial board with an established reputation endorsing the journal.
o   A fast, and friendly, peer review process. This depends on how you work but, having a limited number of submissions, it becomes very feasible.

The above points might be taken as a "promise" that the journal will quickly gain consensus across the scientific community and that the time invested in an article in your journal will bring more, or simply alternative, benefits than the time spent to publish in an already established journal. This might also be facilitated by the fact that perspective authors know you personally and decide to believe in you and your capacities to develop a journal. Credibility may also depend on the approach of the journal and its desire not to shoot too high. Everybody has ambitions, and hopes, that their journal will become a leading one in the field. But there is no need to anticipate this and claim that a newly established journal is (or is bound to be) already a leading one in the field. Sometimes a display of modesty and realistic expectations helps to get credibility amongst your "investors" that are potential authors. I am more likely to give my article to a journal that is aware they are not going to be outstanding but works to be a good one, than to one that aims at being a leading journal but provides little elaboration on its vision.

An article for a new journal is a bit like a donation. Colleagues offer you a donation of some of their time and effort to support a cause. It thus helps a lot if, in addition to believing in you, they believe in the project. Your journal must thus offer something unique, or that was not available before.

Case study—the rising of new academic journals

A colleague, and good friend of mine, recently submitted to a newly established academic journal. I pointed out to him that he would not be able to claim any credits according to his university system. But he had some counter-arguments.

First, the journal was unique in its focus. Until recently, indeed, no other journal had the specific regional coverage of that journal. As a result, the journal was likely to become a major reference for scholars working on that specific region. He would not be able to claim credits, but his article would thus reach the audience he needed it to and he would be able to engage with scholars and experts on the region he is interested in.

Second, the journal was managed by a well-known scholar who was being very active in soliciting articles and, because of his reputation, he could ask people to believe in his project and deliver one article to him.

Third, because the journal was relatively unknown, and independent, it had little pressure from the academic community on what its article should look like. In addition, the editor had asked him personally to write an article and he was expecting to get reviewers that, within respect of a blind peer-review process, would be more sympathetic to his approach. Consequently, he would be able to write an article the way he liked, not the way it should look like to please anonymous reviewers.

Finally, because of so many excellent efforts by the editor in chief, the journal has recently been acquired by a major publisher. He did not know at that time that the publisher would allow access to the journal only for subscribers, thus affecting the visibility of his article. Nonetheless, the fact that a major publisher has acquired the journal could be seen as a sign of quality, that the journal was bound to become a reference and would, at some point, be included in Scopus.

A second colleague submitted an article to a journal showing a similar pattern, although passing through different stages in its brief life. The journal was established fully as open access but with a tough and constructive review process, it had a focus that no other journal offered at that time. It also benefited from excellent connections and an active editorial board that managed to have, as a guest editor for its special issue, one of the leading sociologists in the world.

As a scholar, I might be reluctant to submit an article to a newly established journal. However, if my academic guru, or at least a professor whom I admire, has been guest editing an issue of the journal, I might follow their footsteps and publish there as well. First, their presence might lead me to think that, with the support from their reputation, the journal is likely to take off quickly and become a leading journal in the field. Second, it might be a matter of moral satisfaction to enter an academic outlet where someone who I have admired my whole career has also published.

In both cases, I believe that the editorial board made some good moves and bet on the right horse because both journals are now gaining popularity and, even if not in Scopus, have been increasingly regarded as a reference in the field. It might be that they remain out of Scopus for a long time still, but they would not be the only good journals deciding to stay out of a given database.

The advantages, and traps, of publishing open access

The value of open access publications is, by now, widely acknowledged. It is generally assumed that availability of research findings on the Internet allows scientists from all over the world, no matter how equipped their library is, to have access to your results. In addition, publishing open access is also a way to popularize science in that that anyone interested in your findings, be they from the academic community or not, can download and read your article.

This latter point is a bit ambiguous, I would be curious to see how many people, busy with their day jobs, are willing and have the time to download something 5–10.000 words long, filled with technical words, and read it in their free time. An alternative could be to suggest scientists that each article (or each number of articles) could be summarized into a short blog, post or article (800–1000 words maximum) written in a non-specialized language.

This would be easier to read and digest by non-academics, thus being a good way to make the general public aware of the latest frontiers of research in a given field.

At any rate, when talking about open access, two main options are available.

Option one is to publish in a journal that is fully open access. This means that the journal keeps by default all of its articles freely available and downloadable in a given database (often on the journal's website). This also usually means that the journal has no claims with regards to the commercial exploitation (copyright) of your article.

Copyrights, when speaking of academic articles, can be separated into moral and economic rights. As the author of an intellectual output, you usually maintain full moral rights on your work. This basically means the right to be identified as an author of a given piece of work. Moral rights usually remain to the author(s) of a given work.

By contrast, economic rights refer to the possibility to commercially exploiting a product and receiving money from its sales. When you publish an article with a commercial publisher, you are usually asked to fill out a copyright form and send it back to them. By doing this, you are passing your economic right on the article to the journal, and to the company managing the journal. Basically, you write an article. They sell it and make money from it. For a book, the process is slightly different. You still hand over your economic rights on your academic output, but you receive, in exchange, a compensation in the form of a lump-sum or a percentage of the sales. The company managing the book, however, keeps most of the earnings from your piece of creative work.

Full open access means that the publisher claims no economic rights on your work, that can then be circulated and shared with virtually no limitations, as long as the publisher is acknowledged. This is, in principle, an ideal situation. The problem is that, at least in some disciplines, the number of internationally recognized journals that adopt this model is limited. The majority of journals, in contrast, still offer open access options but in a different way.

Indeed, **Option two** means to publish with a commercial publisher, hand over your economic rights on your article but ask them to make it available for free on their website. By doing this, they incur a loss since they cannot sell it anymore. Consequently, they ask you to indemnify them for an estimated equivalent of their loss, make a calculation of how much they are lacking in earnings (usually a few thousand euros) and bill you for the equivalent.

The process is smooth and makes sense commercially. But there are two oddities.

One is that you work, give your work away for free, some other scholars review your work for free but then you have to pay a company because they cannot commercially exploit the work that you have made at no cost for them.

The other is that, usually, you do not pay yourself to make your work available on open access. You use university funds[12] and many remark that, in most cases, your work is paid for twice (often by taxpayers). If you work in a public university, your salary is at least partly paid by public money and you are paid to produce research. The time you spent on conducting research or experiments, and then write a paper to share the results, is paid for from your salary. If you then want to make your research available publicly, you can pay an open access fee. But this usually comes from your university funds or a research grant (that is public taxpayer's money again).

Even leaving the question on whether this is taxpayer's money aside, your work is paid for twice. It comes to you as a salary only once. The second time the money goes to the company processing your article. It can be argued that this money goes for copy-editing, language editing and other costs but in reality, the amount you pay to "liberate" your article is too high to justify the whole amount you have to pay for open access. There are endless ongoing debates on this.[13] The basic mechanism is that commercial companies provide a service at a price that is ever growing and is possibly too high for what you get.

So, should you publish on open access? Do it if you want, if you have time, if you have research money to pay the publisher to make your article

---

[12] For instance, the European Commission has developed a funding scheme allowing you to apply and get money back if you have paid for making your article open access with a commercial publisher.

[13] You might want to have a look at The researchers.one Mission www.researchers.on e/article/2018-07-1 and Untangling Academic Publishing https://zenodo.org/record/ 546100#.W5O8uhh8Lys

available. However, with the first open access model you are enabling scientists, and anyone interested from all over the world, to access your articles. With the second one you are also helping scientists, and anyone interested/ But you are, at the same time, offering a gift to a private company, helping them earn from your intellectual property (in exchange for the prestige you will get from publishing with that company). You are also supporting a very specific model in science that has little reason to exist. Nowadays, with the Internet and easily accessible layout and design programs, most services that commercial publishers provide can be accessed at an extremely low price. Quality control and assurance mechanisms are also easy to secure by involving in the process established academics and working towards transparency and integrity of procedures. Will it be possible to reduce the role of commercial publishers in the publication process? I am not sure. What I am sure of is that some things can easily be done in a different way.

How to make your work available to everyone even if access is restricted?

When an article is published by an open access publisher, and you keep both your moral and economic rights for your article, you can basically do whatever you want and republish it as much as you want, as long as you respect the rules of the new publishers. By contrast, when you publish an article with a commercial publisher, and hand over your economic rights, you fall into a different exploitation regime with many limitations. There are still, however, some ways to make it available to the general public without having to pay the open access fee.

When you publish with a commercial publisher, you usually receive a link, that you can share with your colleagues, allowing anyone to download the PDF of your article fifty times. This is not much but it allows potentially 50 colleagues of yours to get access to your article immediately. Besides, articles can still be shared privately, for instance within a specialized mailing list designated to a selected public, the equivalent of word of mouth on the Internet.

Most journals have an embargo period (12–24 months usually), after which you can upload the final version of your article onto a private website. For instance, if you have your own website, you can check with the publisher how long you need to wait for but you can eventually make the article available after some time.

It is now widely accepted, and acceptable, that the pre-print version of an article can be uploaded onto your university repository. The pre-print version of an article is the one you receive with the final queries for authors that you need to address before the journal goes into the final publication stage. It is a bit embarrassing to share your typos and imperfections with virtually everyone, but this version (or simply a word version of the article when it was submitted) can be made available from day one at no extra costs.

You can reprint your journal article as a book chapter. This could be of little use if the publisher is again a commercial one and access to your newly published chapter is restricted. At any rate, republishing an article usually entails the payment of a republication fee, unless you are the author or editor of the book, in which case the fee is usually waved. Reprinting, or re-publication, fees also apply if the new chapter is in another language. However, this is a grey area. Translations into languages that are faraway might differ a lot. As a result, the company might find it difficult, or simply not worth it, to prove that the chapter you have just published in Bhutanese is the same one as you have in English in that famous journal of theirs.

You can publish something similar to what has already been published with a commercial publisher as long as there are no more than 400 words in common with the previous publication. However, with up to 800 words in common, publication of a similar work is still possible upon copyright clearance with the first publisher.

Rules might change depending on the company you publish with. The examples above are provided to give you a starting point to then think of the best strategy to maximize the impact of your work while staying within legality.

Case study: some republication strategies

1. A colleague and I edited a special issue of a journal and then a book on the same topic. Our first intention was just to have a special issue, but we received so many promising abstracts that we decided to go for a journal guest issue and an edited book.

The book came out around twelve months after the special issue and all the chapters were original and unpublished. However, when it came to my chapter, I realized that I had no time to write something brand new and started exploring the possibilities I had.

Still, the topic we had used for the article fits perfectly for the scope of the book. It would be thus worth it to use some of the material we had to prepare a chapter. Because the book would target a different audience a similar chapter was an acceptable compromise and it would make our work available to a different segment of the academic community.

We were proposed to apply for permission to re-use up to 800 words from the previous article, but we wanted to avoid applying for copyright clearance (we were late with the book submission and it was unclear how long it would take to get it) so I decided to try a different kind of approach. The article that had been published the year before and had been written three years earlier. It had then undergone two rounds of reviews and had been radically changed both in its empirical and theoretical parts. Technically, the article that was published was radically different from the one that had been submitted.

I took the first submitted version, deleted most of the theory and expanded the empirical part with outputs from the original article. Then added some theoretical notions in the introduction to allow some minimal theoretical contextualization of the study while keeping the focus of the chapter empirical. Once this was done, I sent it to the publisher for a copyright check. They used anti-plagiarism software and the chapter came out clear from any allegation of reuse or plagiarism. In other words, the publisher considered the chapter a different product, with regards to the article, and allowed publication with no clearance.

2. An extremely productive colleague of mine once suggested a perfectly legit strategy to get the maximum output out of an empirical study. When he had, say, a survey administered by three different administrative units (cities, communities, countries, let us call them A, B and C) he would go on and publish a first article with the results of the survey in unit A, a

second article with the results in unit B and one with the results in unit C. Then he would publish comparative studies A-B, A-C and B-C. Finally, he could publish an article comparing A-B-C.

I am not keen to use this strategy myself, but I have to admit that it makes sense. Technically, you are publishing different bits of your study and it is licit to refer to the same theoretical framework, as long as you do not copy and paste the same section into all of your papers. The introduction of all these papers can also refer to a similar theoretical paradigm but it will change according to the empirical data presented in each paper.

3. In a series of less fortunate cases, I have not been able to take advantage of my own work. I am sometimes invited to republish some of it in a language other than English. If I own the economic rights on the article, there is no issue. But when we talk about a piece of work for which I had handed off my economic rights on the article, then the correct thing to do is to apply for a copyright clearance. This means to ask for permission to republish the article in another language and, where applicable, compensate the publisher for the loss incurred. Allegedly, publication in another language means that some potential buyers of the article in English might decide to read it in another language (for free or paying the other outlet) and thus the publisher will earn less.

In practice, I do not see how this could happen if the article is published in Estonian. How many Estonian academics would refrain from buying my article because it has come out in Estonian? According to my calculations, no one. All Estonian universities have already had access to my article via their databases. Having the same article in Estonian would mean that some colleagues might prefer to read it in their native language.

However, to be on the safe side, there is a procedure and my naive hope is that publishers will realize that there is, in fact, no real loss from allowing republication in a minor language. But corporations are difficult to deal with, among other things, because they are so big that they have little time, or desire, to deal with a single case, or an exception. They have their rules and will simply apply them to a standard situation. Republication of an article in my field, in another language, has a standard price, no matter what the potential (lack of) impact it has on the corporation.

Eventually, permission to republish is usually granted but it comes with the request to pay a clearance fee. I have a few reservations on this request and this is why I have never paid anything so far, even if I had the money to do so. First, the article would go into outlets that have very small budgets and do not charge to access their material. Second, usually, the journal offers to translate the text for free, already incurring into a significant cost even without the clearance fee. Third, there is usually no profit to be made from republishing. I reprint in open access journals to make my work available for different audiences. Finally, as mentioned above, there is no real loss for the company and I would have to pay, or fundraise, to be able to use my own work.

At a recent attempt, I have been proposed to pay a discounted publication fee (worth 30 percent of the amount I was supposed to pay). I was moved. I could have paid this amount out of research funds. But how can this expense be morally justified when what I was supposed to pay was the annual budget of the journal I was going to publish in? And what kind of loss would the commercial publisher have to bear if my article was translated and published into Ukrainian for the Ukrainian scientific community? I told my correspondent that I was flattered by their offer to give me a discount, but I would not be able to take them up on it. I understand the commercial logic, and I know that an administrator has no rights to wave my fees. But my question about the legitimacy of such logic remain.

In which database should I try and stand out?

Existence of different metrics to evaluate academic work makes it more complicated to decide where to stand out. Some journals are indexed in a database but not in another and cross-database citations do not count. If your article is in a Scopus journal and someone cites you, Scopus will not pick up your citation unless that other journal is indexed in Scopus.

As a starting point, you should check what is the most important for your national evaluation system, since this is what determines your career path (promotions, grant applications or even capacity to maintain your job). If you plan to apply for a fellowship abroad, you might keep an eye out for what are the evaluation criteria of the host country, and if you should favor a given database, or publication standards, to others. Further to that, I would consider three possible attitudes of databases, and in general ways to assess academic excellence of a scholar: exclusive, exclusive but expanding and all-inclusive.

Exclusive is, at least in my view, the WoS. The database continuously includes new journals, but it does so at a conservative pace. By force of this, it is sometimes considered as delivering better quality assessments of journals and metrics. I remember one specific case when I had applied for a fellowship and I got penalized by the fact that I had a few publications in the WoS, since my primary target had been Scopus.

Exclusive but expanding refers to Scopus. There is a quality control check, but the database has been expanding relatively quickly in the past years *de facto* breaking the quasi-monopoly created by the WoS initially. Because of its inclusiveness, it has become the reference in countries that are attempting to measure, and boost, their scientific excellence, but understand that WoS is too selective and exclusive, at least in some disciplines. In other words, Scopus is a way to put the bar a bit lower and become more inclusive when measuring scientific excellence. But this is also why, at least in some environments, it is no longer sufficient to publish in a Scopus journal. Your journal should fall into a given quartile of Scopus (usually Q1, or at most Q2).

Google Scholar can be referred to as "all inclusive." It is not a database, but it is often used as a proxy to measure scientific excellence of a given scholar or scientific units. Google Scholar has been widely criticized because it picks a scholar's citation regardless of whether their work has been cited in a book, an indexed journal or any other kind of document. If your name is on some document, chances are that Google Scholar will find it and add it to your citations. Google Scholar has also been questioned because it is relatively easy to deceive the algorithm on which it is based and gives extra citations "for free." However, this has been used as a compromise by evaluation systems that see no advantage in being too exclusive or selective. In other words, if I am in charge of measuring scientific excellence in my given country and realize that, by using WoS or even Scopus as a reference, the majority of the scholars of a given country do not have enough publications to be evaluated, I need to find other criteria. This is what has happened in some universities where initial ambitious attempts of measuring excellence have led to the endorsement of a given database. Taking Scopus as a reference, it has turned out that only ten or twenty percent of the researchers in the country (at least for some disciplines) had enough citations to be considered active and of good quality. If one, two or several researchers in my department are below average, I can still replace them, motivate them, and/or give them a grace period. However, if I have criteria to measure excellence and only a couple of scholars meet them, it becomes easier to change the criteria, rather than firing the whole department (or country).

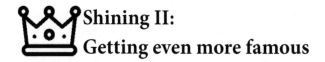# Shining II: Getting even more famous

How to choose the literature to use for an article?

Setting aside a number of seminal works that almost any specialist in a given field will know, each scholar you meet will suggest to you some works you have never heard of. They will claim that this or that book will help you to better develop your research the way you need it. I have a dual position on this. My take is that people will suggest works that will help to develop my research the way they see it but not necessarily as I see it or as I want. However, I have to admit that I have found it very inspirational to mingle with a variety of people who suggest the most different works that perfectly match my research. Not only it broadens my mind and horizons but also allows me to find possible sources of inspiration in studies that I would not have looked otherwise.

At any rate, the advent of the Internet, and especially of academic search engines, has opened a (very large) window on the range of works, related to yours, available worldwide. In principle, this is awesome. If before you needed to go to a library and hope that they have enough works on your topic, now you are submerged by a variety of things that you might want, or need, to cite, and possibly read, to make your study more credible.

There is a two-fold issue that the abundance of literature faces you with and I call it "the hierarchization of literature." You cannot possibly cite everything that is suggested to you and that you find on the Internet. But you can rank them by importance and cite the first X studies from the list you made. This will include your favorite works, those that inspire you. But what about the rest? If you happen to discuss with 20–30 different scholars every year, and each of them suggests 5 works, do you need to add that much to your final bibliography? And can you afford it (in terms of time and space in the paper)?

This operation is even more complicated when you are preparing the literature section for a research grant application. The more literature you insert the less space you have for other sections, that might be more important. On the other hand, a state-of-the-art section that is too short looks bad on an application and you will get, most likely, penalized. As many project writing manuals suggest, the state-of-the-art is simply a way to show that you are aware of the main debates, so you do not need to insert all possible work on the topic. What you need to do is to give priority to the 20–30 works that need to be in the list or the reviewer will think you are not sufficiently knowledgeable on the topic.

Few mention it but virtually everybody knows that reading takes time from other things. As a result, I am not sure that reading from page one to the last page of whatever works or study you are suggested will be a good strategy. You could, of course, take a course in speed reading but even in that case, would you have time to zealously read everything?

Well, I have not and this is why I have come to classify the literature I find during an Internet search into four categories:

1. I am not interested, or this is not sufficiently relevant to what I am writing.
2. I am not particularly interested in the study and it will not change my perception on the topic. I am writing about it, but this is a study so close to what I am doing that I have to at least mention it.
3. Even if I am not necessarily interested in this work, I need to quote it because, by the number of citations it has, I am confident that the reviewer will notice its absence from the literature review. At any rate, let me have a look at the abstract or glance through the paper quickly to see if I need to glance through or read it.
4. This looks interesting and relevant, it could help me sharpen my argument or deepen some aspects of my study. I need to read it.

Eventually, the works you use for your literature review, and the ones you decide to cite, depend upon your strategic choice. Do you prefer to cite the most famous works and have a more mainstream literature review? Or do you balance it with critical and regional studies? If I have to write a literature review for a project application, or for a mainstream journal, I might want to make sure I am not missing out any of the works that are widely considered seminal on a given topic. If I write for a more critical journal, I might want to embrace more of the critical literature, sometimes ignoring seminal works. If I write a book chapter, or for an outlet that has explicitly requested my contribution and I know I will get away with whatever I write, then I might choose to cite mostly, or solely, the things I am a fan of.

In this respect, bibliometrics may be useful for several purposes.

First, if you are a newcomer and need to map the main works in a new discipline, field or topic, your starting question might be "What are the most cited works related to the topic I am writing about?" This says little about the quality of these works, if you will like them or not, and even less about the most important critical works in the field. But it is a starting point and I might be safely confident that most reviewers will agree with my choice. Some might notice that I am missing out on some major critical works, or I do not know some regional studies that are relevant in the region I am studying. But all in all, by citing what other people cite mostly means I have done my homework.

Second, if you are not a newcomer, you might want to cross-check that you are not missing out on any major works. Even if you have been working on a given topic for years, you might have unintentionally overlooked something. Or perhaps you are writing something closely related to your topic but the slight switch in your focus requires you to check if there is anything relevant, or widely cited, on that specific angle that you are taking. You might want to do this also to avoid "reinventing the wheel."

There is a tool that I have used extensively whenever I am unsure on whether I am citing all the works I am expected to cite. Publish or Perish[14] is an (open software) application that you can install on your computer to do a search by author, keywords or a number of other criteria.

You type in an author, one or more keywords and it will display a number of published documents, their authors and the number of times they have been cited. It is by far not the only way you can conduct a search. For one thing, you might just go into Google Scholar or even try one of our famous indexes (Web of Science, Scopus) but the approach is the same.

In addition to the documents whose titles you find intriguing, Publish or Perish allows you to see immediately how many times that work has been cited. If you type in keywords that are highly relevant to your research and some work that has attracted 10.000 citations pop up, it is very likely that

---

[14]   See https://www.harzing.com/resources/publish-or-perish

you will need to cite it in your article. Otherwise, the reviewers might ask why you are ignoring that piece of work that everyone else is citing. You can still destroy the piece but, inasmuch as it looks relevant to the debates you are engaging in, I think that it makes sense to cite it.

By clicking on a title on the list generated by your keywords, you will be directed automatically to the original document, or its page. You can then check the abstract and try to get a sense of whether you really need that article or book. You then compile a long list with the titles, and abstracts, of the works that are most cited and that you have found somehow interesting or relevant to what you are doing. In a next step, you glance through abstracts, articles and other documents to short-list a number of them that will eventually be included in your literature section.

Eventually, this exercise may also give you some inspiration on what keywords, and titles, appear more often, or what titles have caught your attention immediately. Some reflections on the keywords and titles of the paper will also help you to think of better titles for your works, or simply titles that will be easier to find through a Google search and will grab the attention of potential readers.

Publish or Perish, or any other quantitative approach you use, is not a way to replace knowledge, conversations with colleagues or a way to be lazy and do a bibliography in an hour. For one thing, there are books that have an excellent reputation but have come out a year ago and therefore did not gather enough citations to rank high on bibliometrics-based searches. To find out about these books you need to do qualitative searches: word of mouth, mailing lists, by chance and it is part of your job to stay informed on whatever relevant comes out in a year. Nonetheless, this approach can be used to cross-check that you are on the right way and that you are engaging with the works you are supposed to.

One participant of a workshop said that my approach sounds a bit consumeristic. Nonetheless, it is also a way to reduce the risk of neglecting some works that are relevant and useful. You read an abstract, a book review, a synopsis and then make a decision on whether you just need to be aware that the work exists, you need to loosely know its content, or you actually have to read it and engage with it in your paper.

How to locate your paper in current debates (theoretical vs empirical paper)

After the steps above you have a list of sources that you need, or want, to cite in order to publish. Of course, lists change. It's up to your skills to understand what keywords you should use for a given article. Different keywords will give you different outputs and you might want to try a few and discover what is the best combination for the debate you plan to engage in.

In other words, once you have your ingredients, it is time to mix them and prepare a literature review that is synchronized with the rest of the article. Now, which approach you might prefer depends on the outlet you are targeting. I usually classify journals on a spectrum: from fully theoretical to fully empirical. All journals fall somewhere on the continuous line between these two cases.

The more a journal is theoretical, the more they are looking for articles that have a solid theoretical message. This means that the empirics are important only as long as they can confirm, or challenge, some relevant theoretical paradigm, often at the expense of the empirical data to be presented. The underlying message of a theoretical paper may be "We trust that your empirical data are fine, now tell us what this means for fundamental research or for general theory." By contrast, empirical journals will be keener in presenting newly processed empirical evidence and not necessarily interested in identifying immediately their role for general theory. In this case, the message might be "Take care of your evidence, show that data were collected, and processed, in an impeccable way. Then someone else will find out what is their theoretical relevance or where they can be applied to solve some major theoretical problem."

Your literature review will be composed of:

1. works dealing with fundamental research and general theory of the discipline you are based in
2. empirical studies on similar topics
3. competing works (similar research conducted on different samples, regions of the world, or subjects).

The literature part of a theoretical paper will have to mention numbers 3 and 2 but only inasmuch as they help you to contextualize your paper and explain its relevance for number 1. The more you move towards an empirical paper, the more you will need to emphasize number 3 while minimizing 1. In some cases, a paper that presents brand new data could simply ignore points 1, 2 and 3 and simply concentrate on the methodology for its data collection, or the results of an experiment, with the understanding that some other scholars, in the future, will use the data to propose some theoretical conclusions.

In addition, my understanding of academic debates is that, for every topic, you will have a position 1 (or A) that has been endorsed by a number of scientists, and studies. This position has been considered solid until someone has come up with a position 2 (or B) that significantly challenges 1 and can be seen as its antithesis. All further studies will have then to endorse A or B, placing themselves on a spectrum between the two (fully reject A to then endorse B; or suggest that A is insufficient to understand a given phenomenon). At some point, someone will come up with a position C that will change the power of dynamics between A and B and (replace A or B and find a synthesis of the two) so that the new debate will then start from A and C or B and C.

Once you identify your A and B, you can start building your jigsaw and locate each of the studies you want to cite with regards to A, or B. By doing this, you are implicitly working towards the main argument of your paper. You explain what studies relate to A and B and why they succeeded, or failed, to answer a given question. As a result, you might eventually see how the contribution of your paper adds to the debates.

During a workshop, I initiated an exercise: to take the same topic and frame it in three different papers, from a fully empirical to a fully theoretical one. Let us take a study on identity in Ukraine. How could you frame it?

Fully theoretical article

A number of studies on identity have suggested that it is mostly influenced by factors like...and (position 1). In contrast, a number of recent works have pointed at further possible elements influencing identity formation, namely (position 2).

This article uses empirical evidence drawn in Ukraine to question position 1 and suggest that position 2 is possibly more relevant.

Empirical article

Identity in Ukraine has long been debated. While some scholars have tended to look at (position 1), some other scholars have concentrated on (position 2) as more relevant. This article provides further evidence to support position (1 or 2) by showing that.

A more extreme variation of the above might be to simply present the results of a survey or any other empirical evidence gathering data on identity in Ukraine. To me, this could be more adapt as a book chapter but some journals (with Ukraine as its main focus) might be happy to take it as is.

Somewhere mid-way between empirical and theoretical (area studies)

Debates on identity formation in the former USSR region have tended to concentrate on (position 1) and on (position 2). Both positions have been regarded as exceptions to theoretical paradigms suggesting...This article endorses (or challenges) these positions (or one of them) by using empirical evidence to suggest that...

In the end, your paper is an exercise of synchronizing all its section's parts. It is very easy to reject the paper if you see that the introduction is promising the moon, and then the empirical part is not doing much. You may know theory well but be deficient in empirics or the other way around. In a good article, you need not to show that you know everything. You simply need to know enough to explain the relationship between the variables that you have chosen. There is a point that I call a saturation point after which any other information is not adding anything or is adding so little that you do not really need it.

Before submitting to a journal, it might be worth to see what kind of articles they publish to understand the potential interest not only in your topic but also in your (theoretical vs empirical) approach. Some journals openly prefer empirical articles while others theoretical ones. Finally, do not forget that reviewers are human beings and they might not know, understand or like your topic. You have better chances if you submit to a journal that has published things similar to your research in the past.

Why (not) to publish with Cambridge University Press?

Virtually everyone knows Cambridge University Press and its value, in academic terms. In the past years, a new publisher has been emerging using the Cambridge label. Cambridge Scholars Publishers (CSP) is a company based in Newcastle founded by a group of Cambridge graduates. They solicit books from scholars, junior and senior, from a variety of world regions. Their entrepreneurial approach has eventually been prized and there are a large number of academics now publishing with them. A few colleagues were contacted with the request to consider them for a future book they might be writing, or editing, or to publish the proceedings of a conference they were organizing at the time.

What do you do when this happens? Should you publish with them? My answer, as usual, is that it depends on your national evaluation system and on your ambitions. In a number of national evaluation exercises, CSP, like many others, is considered a decent publisher. You publish with them and you get credits for your book. Colleagues in some countries have told me that they can claim credit as long as their book is in English, with little difference on who the publisher is. If so, why not to go with CSP?

What becomes a bit more complicated is to claim credit not from your national evaluation system but amongst the academic community. If you go to a major conference and sign your book off with a publisher like CSP, I am not sure about the amount of credit you will get from your audience and colleagues, but I suspect, it is less than you could claim if your book was with Cambridge University Press.

At a lower level on the scale of academic prestige, there are a number of vanity or predatory publishers that have been growing in the past years. I consider predatory any publisher that goes around soliciting manuscripts for the simple reason to make a profit out of it with no interest whatsoever in the quality of the final output. This eventually affects the quality of the manuscripts both academically (since there is no peer review) and technically (often copy editing is not performed or even the layout is of low quality). Vanity publishers move on the same territory and they mainly target scholars, or in general people, who are happy by simply having their name on any manuscript.

When I finished my PhD, I was contacted by a publisher named Presses universitaires européennes with an offer to publish my PhD thesis. Since the name of the press sounded solid I was tempted. After all, my thesis was in French already and I knew I would not publish it as a book in English because its chapters were too inconsistent. But this is why a book in French, with a publisher that sounded solid, could be an asset on my CV. I was moving across the English speaking world and the probability that a potential employer would check my thesis in French was low. As long as the publisher had an appealing name, it could be assumed that my book was somehow of acceptable quality.

The deal breaker, however, came relatively quickly. I warned them that French was not my native language and the manuscript had to at least go through some copy editing before publication. The answer of the publisher was that they trusted me as an author and they would publish my manuscript as it is. The expert had gone through my book and had decided that it was of the highest possible quality. Anyone, even native speakers, makes typos and little mistakes. Why would they think I was immune from that? I had to retrieve all my critical spirit and think like Groucho Marx, "I would never enter a club that accepts me among its members." I also did some research on the Internet and found out that I was most likely dealing with an emerging predatory publisher. This meant that, even if virtually unknown at that time, within a few years they would become notorious among the academic community and I would have to hide the publication from my CV. I stopped replying to their emails and never published my dissertation, a thing I have not regretted yet.

The lesson I learned from this adventure is that efforts and results should be proportionate. The higher you target, the better the quality you need to deliver, the harder you need to work. But if your national evaluation system does not credit you for a book with the best publisher, and you just need a monograph to confirm your position, maybe targeting the best publisher ever is not worth the effort. Whatever publisher you target, you should be able to defend your choice in the future. The list of vanity publishers is constantly changing and presses that are considered decent in one country might have a bad reputation in another. It is, therefore, better to check twice and do not go below a certain level of quality to avoid getting in trouble at a later stage of your career.

Plus and minuses of working with someone very famous

Getting published is already a merit in itself since it means you are able to produce something worth the attention of a journal. But between publishing and getting recognized by the academic community, there is still a long way to go. There is not one but many excellent journals in your field and they all publish several articles per year. Why should someone be willing to read what you have written instead of what someone else, perhaps more famous than you are, has published in the same period?

As a PhD student, the first opportunity you have to stand out in a crowd is to use your PhD supervisor(s) channels. As a general rule, during your PhD, you need to be supervised by an established scholar and learn from them. As a friend once said, "We are craftsmen, we learn our job from someone who teaches us and this is why it is necessary to choose your supervisor well." Your supervisor is not only your advisor for academic matters but should also be the first person to turn to when you need strategic advice on where to publish or where to apply for a job.

Being supervised by someone extremely skilled might make your life easier in many ways. For one thing, co-authoring with your supervisor will immediately expose you to their public and possibly receive a few citations. If your supervisor regularly writes for a blog, a newspaper or a magazine, they might at some point invite you to co-author an entry or an article. They might also ask you to write an article yourself, once they think your writing skills have sufficiently developed, or if they think this could, in fact, be a good exercise. In a similar fashion, the day some radio or TV journalists need your advisor and they cannot go, they might ask you to go in their place. You could become their junior assistant when advising a government or an international organization and work with them for years, or even be contacted directly once someone needs a consultant and ask your advisor whom to contact.

However, working with someone extremely famous is like being a child of a very famous parent. Your road might be easier but the shadow of your parent will always be there. Because your supervisor is not your father or mother, you have the choice of how closely to follow their path and go behind them. Inasmuch as this is useful and gives you a fast track in a number of cases, it might be deleterious in the long run so finding a balance between dependence and autonomy might be a good idea.

Arrange guest lectures

In my dream world I am sitting in my room reflecting on some fundamental questions about science and then I receive a call. Someone needs me to deliver a lecture on something and are ready to arrange everything for me to be there. I am not excluding that, at some stage of your career, you will fit into this superhero-like scenario. But it might be a long way off before that happens.

Until then, guest lectures are usually the result of chance. A paper that you have published at the right moment in the right journal, a casual encounter at a conference or on the Internet. I once saw on LinkedIn someone looking for guest speakers and I contacted her. To my surprise, she invited me to deliver a speech at her department's lunch seminar series and paid for everything.

As a scholar, you need guest lectures for at least three reasons.

First, in a number of cases, you are requested to mention on your CV where you have delivered speeches (the higher the university ranks, the better it looks on your CV).

Second, a guest lecture is the equivalent to word of mouth in academia: you engage with a relatively small public (smaller than your potential readers if you published on an Internet blog) but interaction is more intense and engaging.

Third, it allows you to get feedback from different publics, scholars from other disciplines or individuals simply unfamiliar with your work. If they like you as a person, it is more likely that they will retain your name and read, or at least notice, your next publications.

A guest lecture has no standard format. At one extreme of the spectrum, there is you delivering a speech in front of ten thousand people at a major event where you are flown in in business class and everything is arranged around you. At the other extreme, you just walk next door from your university (for instance, if your city has two universities) and talk in front of

10–15 colleagues who have never heard of your work (except, perhaps, the one who has invited you to their university).

A guest lecture can be arranged easily and the only pre-requisite is to have someone in the guest institute who thinks it is a good idea to have you over. They can be arranged in the frame of a fellowship you are holding at another university, in a neighboring town, after a conference you have attended at a university, if you stay one or two extra days. They can, of course, result from an invitation from a colleague who has found you through an Internet search and who has funds to invite you. But they can also be done in the course of a journey or a holiday (but make sure the people you are going on holiday with are not against it). You have a colleague working in a city that you need to visit anyway. Your colleague could find a room, some snacks and circulate the message throughout their university.

Attend conferences and international events

This might sound banal since we have all thought that we have to present at conferences from the very early years of our PhD, or even master's degree. But there are different ways to land, and attitudes to engage with, in a conference environment. What is the best possible outcome from a conference presentation? Two things, I would say.

One is that your panel is super crowded. You had just submitted an abstract and end up in the panel with the most famous person in the field. From there, it is all in your hands. You deliver a clear, interesting and dynamic presentation and gain a substantial number of (academic) fans who retain your name and will read your work, or even invite you to collaborate in the future.

The other one is that you meet some colleagues during social events, like a networking dinner or coffee breaks, get along with them and decide to start a collaboration.

It is possible that either outcome will be the result of chance—or luck, as I see it. But what are the odds that this will happen with no effort from your side? If you are relatively unknown, you are rather likely to end up in some anonymous panel, sometimes at the last session on the last day. What are the ways you can maximize the final outcome of your participation?

Choose the right conference. The closer the event to your research interest the more likely you are to find people with similar professional affinities. Besides, if you have some kind of reputation in a given discipline, field or subfield, chances are that you will be put in a panel where you will receive more attention. I recently attended a conference where my topic did not really fit in and my presentation was scheduled for the last panel on the last day. We were still lucky to have five people listening but sometimes you might have to present in an empty room.

Be active with the professional association organizing the conference, or at least try to start some collaborations with some members of the board. If the organizers know you, they might entrust you with some tasks and you will have the chance to meet more people and get a better time slot, or panel, at the conference.

Socialize at the book exhibition, wine receptions or other social events, excursions, conference dinner and coffee breaks. Academics are human beings and they like to relax like everyone else. You might end up sitting at the same table with your future employer or chatting about mundane things with your next co-author.

Contribute to the scientific program. This may range from acting as a section chair, and thus have to manage several dozens of presentations, to simply submit a panel and work with four or five more people. This will give you a starting base of people who you already know. You can then tap from their network, count on their fans to show up at your panel. Alternatively, submit a paper, or a panel, with someone more established than you are. You might end up doing most of the administrative work for them, but your panel is likely to attract better papers and have a few extra people by force of the fame of your co-organizer.

Study the conference program and decide in advance with whom you want to meet. If you have someone in mind that you want to talk to, you can go to their presentation. Over the years I have been surprised by how many people I did not expect to meet (and whose existence I ignored) became good colleagues or even friends simply because I met them at a conference and we liked each other. In the end, if someone likes you as a person it is more likely that they will get interested in your work, cite you, and propose collaborations in the future. This is why for me conferences are not just an excuse to present my work but a chance to meet people. In fact, this latter aspect has become even more important than the former.

Media engagement and popular science books

Non-academic articles are, in principle, not part of your work duties. An increasing number of universities is formally stating that public engagement of researchers is required but they do not necessarily complement this statement with an integrated mechanism allowing you to claim credit for short articles not targeting the academic community. If you are short of time, you concentrate on what is essential to your survival and short pieces for the general public are definitely not what you need to advance in your career. Public engagement through media can also pass through radio and TV interviews, participation in talk shows and other kinds of broadcasting. Also, in this case, not much of your job description points to the fact that you should be engaging in these activities. However, they bring a number of similar advantages with the added value of targeting an even broader audience, especially if you appear on TV at dinner time, or when large audiences are in front of the cathodic tube.

Public engagement has several intrinsic advantages:

More and more varied people will read them. Not everyone will have the time to read your 5–10.000 word article. When you do not have time to read a whole article you can at least check its abstract. However, a short 800–1000 word article might be more attractive and takes a little more time to fast read it than an abstract.

You can count on colleagues reading you with a different mindset (if they find a short article in a newspaper). If someone's work is to read articles, then reading newspapers and magazines is usually a hobby, or something they do in their leisure time (or when taking a break from your work). By publishing an article in a non-academic outlet, you are targeting a different moment of the day. You are not asking them to read you because your study is relevant for their work. You are suggesting that it might be fun to read you in their free time.

Let us imagine an academic that opens a newspaper when taking a break from their work. To take a real break from their life, one could imagine that they decide to read gossip magazines or yellow press. But it is rarely so and

I would bet that, by my working habits, I might be drawn to something somehow related to my work if my eye falls on it when reading a newspaper.

If your article is written in a fluid and captivating style, they might even read it until the end and get to know you as a non-academic author and then end up appreciating you as an academic. What is even more interesting is that, by reading your short article based on a study of yours, they might end up paying more attention to it than they would do had they encountered your abstract somewhere. Once they find it interesting, they will take it into account, remember you and possibly cite it in their next article. This, in spite of not having read your article during their work time (or not having read it at all).

They can be regarded as your moral duty. Once a colleague told me, "You are the specialists in the field. If you are not explaining to society what is happening, who is doing that?" Indeed, academics are qualified to talk, with a certain knowledge, on some topics they have studied for years. If we are not the one informing the public, or politicians who have then to make decisions on evidence-based policies, then who else can do that? When something happens, the media will look for people who could speak with authority and you are, at least in theory, one of those people. In addition to being gratifying, this can also be regarded as a moral duty.

Indeed, when something relevant happens, journalists are looking for specialists to explain to the public what is happening. This lacking, they have to understand it themselves and then explain it but if they have not covered that topic, they cannot become specialists overnight.

Donor's pressure. A growing number of donors are asking us not to keep our knowledge secret in our ivory towers but to share it with the public. Public dissemination has almost become a formal requirement for a number of funding schemes, meaning that you do not have to promise this in your bid but, if you do not do it, chances are that someone else (who has promised to publish public dissemination pieces) will get it in your place.

Visibility. Public servants, workers of international organizations and private companies do not necessarily read academic articles. But it is fair to assume that, to various degrees, they read newspapers and magazines. Being published in media outlets gives you an extra visibility that might lead someone to hire you as a consultant, or simply request your advice.

Depending on your agreement with your university, this might bring you extra money, prestige, freedom or all of them.

Commercial value for a university. Even in systems that do not give formal credits for short articles, engaging with the public brings visibility to your university. If you are known for short opinion articles in the press, some of the people who read you might want to study with you or might want their children to study with you. Because funding, both public and private, depends in part on the number of students you attract, your department, and university, will be happy to have someone who is widely known. Even if it is not possible to measure the impact of one of your articles on the number of people enrolling for a degree in your faculty, there is a general attitude suggesting that articles bring publicity, and thus students.

Your research can also be explained in a longer format, for instance, a popular science book. I am thinking here "The Dictator's Handbook," which is written in a pleasant style and is full of interesting facts, but it is also based on a much more rigorous study published as a 500-page book. I have recently also enjoyed "Predictably Irrational" and "Freakonomics," both based on solid empirical works but narrated in such an easy way that I bought them to read them in my free time. Still, they are well referenced so that I can get back to the studies they cite and eventually use them for my own work.

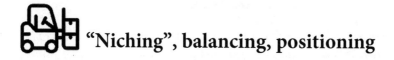 # "Niching", balancing, positioning

PhD: one name, many meanings

There is widespread consensus that having a PhD is a milestone in your academic career. However, what having a PhD means, and entails, can significantly change depending on how you got it.

Think of the case of someone with a full scholarship who completes in 3–4 years devoting themselves fully to a single research project. Think now of someone with no scholarship or who completes in 7–8 years, having already worked in several universities, working to different projects at the same time. For these two academics PhD has a different meaning. One enters the job market with much less experience, publications, collaborations and, in turn, a given vision of the world. The main competitive advantage, in this case, is the capacity to finish a PhD quickly and perhaps the merits associated with receiving a scholarship for PhD studies. The other will probably have a much more extensive CV, experience and collaborations. It took them longer to complete their PhD, perhaps they have found it difficult to survive their PhD years and have taken up several different jobs. But their experience is wider, and they are more likely to have acquired a number of complementary skills in the process.

Who you are at the end of your PhD depends also on your supervisor and on the institutional context. In a more conservative environment, you will be requested to work only on your academic skills and on your topic. A more progressive view on PhD studies will include a series of trainings offering you the chance to develop some additional skills. Some universities require you to write a PhD as some kind of monograph. By contrast, some others follow a "PhD by publication" model. This means that you need to publish your chapters as journal articles and then pull them together, add an introduction and conclusion section, and have a PhD thesis ready.

Given the diversity of available options, and the variety of career patterns, it is not possible to forecast who you will be at the end of the process. It depends on your personal path, the time that you devote to it, and the strategy you opt for in each particular situation.

However, some recent tendencies suggest that PhD theses are now:

Shorter. PhD studies tend to be shorter than some years ago in a number of countries. This is due to the influence of donors, providing funding for a given number of years (usually three or four) and their pressure to see results as quickly as possible. It is also due to the fact that, in a number of cases, funding to public universities is allocated by the number of PhD students who have successfully defended in the last X number of years. In this case, PhD students are under pressure to finish, and quickly, and so are their universities. I know of cases where departments are fined if their students do not complete within a given number of years.

Lighter. Because there is a general interest in producing PhD students, PhD programs have become, in a number of cases, lighter. A case limit could be the replacement, by a much shorter cycle of studies, of the French *doctorat d'Etat* that was considered normal to carry on for years, often up to ten, to make sure that the candidate ended their degree with a vast array of experience. A shorter, and lighter, PhD training gives you the degree required and some competences that can be used in the job market. However, with programs getting easier to complete, all the additional assets that you might need have to be acquired individually and separately. This could happen, perhaps, during a post-doctoral fellowship, taking a longer time to finalize your PhD training path or investing in a series of external trainings. It becomes, thus, a quest to get the best trade-off between speed and quality (of the PhD) and publications and other skills collected during the process.

Applied. Research conducted during PhD programs tends to be more and more applied, as opposed to fundamental, or fully theoretical, one. This is a result of the growing number of PhD scholarships offered and financed externally. Not only do donors want to see some concrete application, or applicability, of the research they have funded. They also might have an interest in a given topic or expect that their funding will help solve some societal challenges. In such cases, research should address a concrete issue that is considered urgent in a given environment or society.

Starting point. A PhD becomes thus a condition necessary but not sufficient to compete in the job market. It offers you the formal qualifications to call yourself a doctor[15] and to apply for a job (although there are cases of researchers who have been hired before their completion). But a PhD only lands you a job where you have to compete with other PhD graduates with other career paths, different merits and assets. You will have to emerge thanks to merits that you have collected along with, or after, your PhD studies.

Besides, the academic community is relatively open to listening to new opinions even if they come from a PhD student. This means that you could start publishing something relatively significant before becoming a doctor. But the general perception of your work, and of yourself, might be affected to various degrees (depending on the country, the discipline, etc.) by whether you have a PhD or not.

With a PhD in hand, you have in principle the authority to speak. It is your call then to decide in what to invest in and what assets to develop. You might use your PhD to attempt a standard career path, but you could use it to sound more authoritative when carrying out consultancy work or working as an analyst. It could even be something you use to then specialize in popularization of science. You take advantage of your title and recently acquired analytical skills to translate the latest research findings into a more accessible language and make it easier for larger audiences to understand.

Each specialization has its advantages and its challenges. The narrower your field is the smaller the competition. If you have studied ancient Aramaic language you could, at least theoretically, be the only candidate for a job. But this does not happen often. You might need to wait that someone opens a position in such an exotic field and it might take years. On the other hand, a broad specialization like "political economy" allows you to apply for a large variety of jobs. It is also likely that competition for each of the positions you want to apply for will be much fiercer.

When the Soviet Union broke up, the paucity of local specialists and need to quickly find ways to invest money in the region contributed to the career of many Russians. Whoever could speak some English, got in touch with foreign investors and promised to help solve some problems was rewarded with huge power, and money. Careers have been built on this path. Some

---

[15] Except in cases such as Germany, where you need to publish your thesis before you are formally awarded the Dr. title.

local academics have eventually changed careers, and possibly cars and homes, given the amount of money they were able to make by simply being in the right place at the right time.[16]

How can you claim credit (and what credit) for your publications?

To answer this question, one should first decide where, and with whom, credit for publications should be claimed. The amount and level of recognition you might get from the academic community and from the institutions in charge of your work performances may differ quite a lot. In the end, what you can claim depends on where you are based (academically and physically), where you want your credit and what is your discipline. Think of journals in the humanities, their slow turnover and the lower level of citations people in the humanities have if compared to science. By contrast, fields such as medicine or biology have a much faster turnaround time.

This also means that expectations are different across countries. Some years ago, I applied for a position and a colleague told me that the number of citations I had on Google Scholar were worth mentioning in the application because it was higher than the number of citations many more senior colleagues managed to have. However, this was her perception from a discipline that was "slow" and in a country where the average academic was not very visible internationally. A similar amount of citations would be considered extremely low in the same country but in another discipline, or in a different country, where the social sciences and humanities had a more international profile.

Think of the European Research Index of Humanities (ERIH) and the reasons for establishing such a database. Before the emergence of the Scopus database, most of academic performance and journals were assessed on the basis of bibliometrics provided by Thomson and Reuters' WoS database, which is fairly comprehensive with regards to science journals but limited with the amount of social science journals included. However, if social science scholars could moan about a few journals missing from the WoS

---

[16]   See Janine Wedel (1998) Collision and Collusion: The Strange Case of Western Age to Eastern Europe, 1990–1997, London: Palgrave MacMillan.

database, humanities scholars were in a worse situation. Few journals in the humanities had the number of citations to be comfortably included in ISI and there was no real reference in the humanities to tell good from less good journals. ERIH was created, thus, to have a starting reference to evaluate humanities scholars but it is nothing but a list of journals that "deserve" to be considered of higher quality. The idea behind it was that an article published in an ERIH-listed journal is of sufficiently good quality to allow its author to claim credit for it.

Case—The traps of diversity of academic evaluation systems

In the absence of any other references, the idea behind the creation of ERIH is, in principle, an excellent one. However, its applicability depends on how widely used the database becomes. In Estonia, ERIH was taken almost immediately as a reference by the ministry and articles published in their journal were considered, by default, first-class ones. It is thus possible to conceive a career based on publications in ERIH journals. This means, in the end, that hard science people will use ISI as a reference and people in the humanities, and sometimes social sciences, will use ERIH.

The problem emerges, however, when you want to go international. After some time in Estonia, I applied for a fellowship in Spain and I was penalized for the insufficient amount of relevant publications I had. When I asked for an explanation, I was told that their standard reference was ISI and that journals not indexed in the Web of Science were not considered sufficiently relevant for them. I found this extremely odd since Scopus was in its ascending phase at that time and I expected that they could use it for the social sciences. However, when the results were finally published, I made sense of this idiosyncrasy. More than ninety percent of the fellowships had gone to science people. Obviously, if your priority is to attract hard science scholars, and you give away a handful of fellowships to the social sciences to claim that scholars from any discipline may apply, you do not really need anything else but ISI. Why bother including anything else?

In principle, if you target only journals that are Q1 in ISI, you should be in a safer position to be able to compete in virtually any markets and any disciplines. But there are at least two pitfalls in this approach.

First, how many people are always able to publish at a Q1 level and always everywhere? Or even just prioritize Q1 journals? This is certainly a strategy to be in the hall of fame of world scholars for but is not widely applicable and probably leaves you little time for a personal life.

Second, there are still systems where this would not work. If a country has a very low research performance, its quality control institutions will need to lower the threshold for academic quality. While this is understandable, it might lead to the situation where the best researchers in the country end up underperforming, when compared with others. Getting an article accepted in a Q1 journal takes in average takes longer than getting it accepted in a non-Scopus or non-ISI journal. As a result, those submitting to non-Q1 journals would be in the position of publishing several articles per year. In contrast, those targeting Q1 journals will probably end up publishing less (but better quality) than the others. If the quality control institution counts only the number of articles produced by each scientist, then those targeting the best (and slower) journals might be regarded as less productive, in spite of benefiting from a better reputation in the academic community.

There is another possible paradox. Italy has recently instituted a commission for the evaluation of academic excellence that was in charge of creating a list of journals[17] that could be considered first class for each discipline. Articles in any of the journals from that list are a priority for academics to be hired, and then promoted, up to the professor level. In principle, this is an excellent (although costly) idea: to mix international standards and start from recognized databases and journals of national relevance. But a separate list has been created for each discipline. If, as a sociologist, you happen to publish a paper with some biologists in a

---

[17] http://www.anvur.it/attivita/classificazione-delle-riviste/classificazione-delle-riviste-ai-fini-d ellabilitazione-scientifica-nazionale/elenchi-di-riviste-scientifiche-e-di-classe-a/

biology journal, you will not be able to claim credit for it. For cognate disciplines, for instance political science and sociology, the situation is the same: you publish in a sociology journal and cannot claim the publication when applying for a political science post. I was told that you can still write to the commission and propose to include a journal in the list. But there is no guarantee that this will happen and, even if in the end it does, the process might be slow. Think of the case where you are applying for a post in sociology and notice that a journal where you have published is included only in the anthropology list, you can ask the commission to include it also in sociology, but that will probably be done after the competition for that post has been concluded.

An example of a more inclusive evaluation system is Estonia's, where ISI and ERIH were initially taken as indicators of academic excellence. Because ERIH was relatively inclusive, there were a few articles I could claim credit for because they were included in it, in spite of not being only humanities journals. But then ERIH could be regarded as too inclusive since I was able to find also journals that, although considered excellent in their field, were not peer-reviewed. Things have changed now, and Scopus is now taken into account by the Estonian ministry as a guarantee of quality. This is to say that you cannot possibly use a one-size-fits-all strategy and expect to become competitive in all possible environments.

Besides, I would say that reputation still counts. Your promotion, tenure or other, will not depend only on formal criteria. The more you have people in the evaluation committee who consider you an excellent scholar, the easier it will be to overcome any obstacles (i.e., you fail to meet one of the formal requirements, or someone in the committee is strongly against you). From your ministry's perspective, an article in a top Q1 journal might be worth as much as an article in the lowest quartile from the same database or even any other journal. But there are other criteria that are not always measurable or tangible such as people who actually enjoy your writings, think you do what you do well or think it is fun to work with you. In the end, when you apply for a position, or simply want the academic community to recognize that your latest book is worth reading, you should have a "capital of reputation" associated with your name. To achieve this, you do not need to meet the ministry's criteria but should think about convincing the people around you, in your field or working in the geographical region of your choice, that your work is worth attention. You should take part in one or more debates, regularly read your colleagues' work and be read by colleagues. This is not a box-ticking exercise, I think it is as important as meeting the formal criteria for a position.

Research, teaching, administration, fundraising: carving your way into stability

So, you finally have got a job. You have been selected by a decent university as a lecturer. But you know that your position is not solid. You are the newest person in the team and need to prove yourself. This means to demonstrate that you are worth the trust they have granted you and that you can perform no worse than anyone else in the department.

Well, if you want to survive, you do not necessarily have to be the best in the department. Remember that in a pack of antelopes chased by a leopard you do not need to be the fastest one. It is sufficient to be the penultimate so that then the leopard will eat the one behind you and leave you in peace. By the same token, to survive in a department, it will be sufficient for you not to be the worst so that, if a few heads fall, yours will not be amongst them.

One of the ways to do this is to build a profile for yourself within the department. But how?

When you entered the academic world, you probably thought that you would have to teach and do research, maybe there would be some boring meetings to attend but that was it. And then you could do anything else you wanted. You had seen some academics writing in newspapers, sitting on committees, consulting governments and so on. But were you aware that you would be supposed to do all of this and more? Peer review, public dissemination, funding applications, editing, evaluation, organizing conferences, international panels, being active in professional organizations are all part of the game. And you are supposed to engage with most, not to say, all of these activities. But were you warned before? Or are they part of the formal duties listed in your contract?

They are not. But if everyone around you is doing something and you are not, would you not feel the pressure to do the same? How could you justify to your boss, to your colleagues or even to yourself, that everyone is sitting on some sort of boring committee and you are not? If you are the only one not doing something, your colleagues might quickly ostracize you, even more, if you are the new one.

But perhaps the worst threat will not come from your colleagues who despise you but rather from the ones who like you. They will be the ones who genuinely believe in the advice they give you when you ask them how they got tenure. The problem is that, as it has been brilliantly illustrated by Radhika Nagapal,[18] your nice colleagues, in an attempt to help you, will destroy your moral. They will suggest you do things that they have done, that they were advised to do but did not because they did not have enough time and those are the things that they realized only years after that they should have done. In other words, the advice given to you will be to do three times the amount of things that they did. Of course, their advice is meant to be in good faith and with the best of intentions. But multiply this by the number of senior colleagues you ask for advice and you have enough suggestions to end up with an unprecedented burnout.

In my view, the only way to tenure is to become indispensable to your department. Well, as they say, everyone is needed but no one is replaceable so indispensable is perhaps a big word. Let us say that you should become someone that is too difficult, or too costly, to get rid of or replace. If you bring a unique, and previously absent, asset into a department, and your colleagues realize this, then firing or replacing you becomes extremely difficult even if you underperform in other work-related tasks. The more your abilities are unique, the harder it is to replace you, the more you can negotiate and decide yourself what to do it, and what not to do. This can happen through open negotiations or simply by a tacit agreement.

By no means does this mean that you become untouchable. If you kill a colleague it is very likely that, even if you are the best scientist in the world, they will have to dismiss you. But, the more you are vital to the department, the easier will be for you to stay even if you are weaker than many other colleagues in some tasks.

For example, if you are a Nobel Prize winner, what are the odds that your line manager will complain about you not bringing enough visibility to the

---

[18] https://blogs.scientificamerican.com/guest-blog/the-awesomest-7-year-postdoc-or-how-i-learned-to-stop-worrying-and-love-the-tenure-track-faculty-life/

university? And if, as a Nobel Prize winner, students complain about you not being a good teacher, would the administration listen to them? A Nobel Prize is a Nobel Prize and their value lays in well beyond their research and teaching performances. They mean visibility, publicity, fame, prestige. You do not fire a Nobel Prize winner unless you have a really good reason for it.

There is only one Nobel Prize per year and not even in all disciplines and it is likely that you will not be amongst them. But there are other ways you can find a place in your department and they all depend on where you have little or no competition. For instance, excellent management and administration skills means that you can take care of management tasks much faster than most of your colleagues. You could then propose to be the department head, or administrator, for many years. In exchange, you could ask for some release from teaching or understanding that your publications are not as good as the ones from colleagues with fewer responsibilities.

Some time ago I found a way that was a de facto buy off. I would agree to teach any course they asked me to teach, usually something that none of my colleagues was interested in delivering. In exchange, I asked to be able to decide my own teaching schedule and teach only compact modules. Having only elective courses and students no one else wanted made my teaching duties far from pleasant, and this is why at some point I broke the agreement. But, apart from this, my life was relatively quiet, and nobody bothered me with other requests.

At a doctoral school in the UK a colleague once said, "If you are a bad teacher and a good researcher, you can get away with that. If you are the opposite, a good teacher and a bad researcher, you will probably not." This is because at the regular research assessment exercise, held in the UK every five or six years, low-quality research will result in a lower score and, consequently, lower public funding for the upcoming years. Eventually, you do not want to be the reason why your department lost 20.000 GBP per year for the next five years. On the other side of the spectrum, however, there are universities whose major source of income are tuition fees from the students. These need to give priority to students' satisfaction so they might prefer a good teacher to a good researcher and turn a blind eye if your students love you, but your research performance is lower than that of most of your colleagues.

Excellent research performance might make up for bad teaching and vice versa, capacity to attract public funding, from the public or business sector, and to manage them might make up for both. If all of your books are best sellers, you have the highest amount of citations out of the whole faculty and this is a priority for the university, you will be regarded as a golden bird. Media presence might be welcomed by universities that need to market themselves and already have enough researchers to show high research performance. Willingness to pursue a management or political career within your faculty or university, especially if you perform well, might mean a significant relief from your teaching and research duties. From the bureaucratic standpoint, you cannot possibly be excellent in all aspects of academia in which you are supposed to excel. But you can pull together a unique combination of skills and performativity to make the management satisfied with you. This means to make them think that you are contributing something substantial to the management, and development, of an academic unit.

All this is extremely unstable, but so is life. If your department head changes, the priorities of the department might also change, and your skills might not be as vital as they were before. Likewise, if the university policy changes, and your abilities do not bring any competitive advantage to your research group or department, you might find it challenging to sell yourself using the same skills you used before. Another possibility is that, at some point, someone with stronger skills than you in one of your specializations is hired. If so, you might lose your monopolistic position and no longer be the only one capable of completing that particular task. But you might still be needed, and an oligopoly is not too different from a monopoly, in some cases. You can rule for ages relatively untouched if you shine above everyone else for some particular skills or abilities.

Is it better to publish a book or a journal?

To some, especially from the social sciences and humanities, this question might sound odd, and the answer might seem obvious. A book is longer, and you are more likely to become "famous" as "the author of that excellent book about..." than as an author of an article. A book entails an editorial project, a contract, negotiations, personalized dissemination channels and strategies. You cannot organize an article launch but you can definitely do a book launch. So why still discuss what is better?

Even the argument "a book is more time consuming" might be questioned. A friend recently told me that he finds the amount of time and efforts devoted to a good article and to a book almost the same. For the book, however, he does not need to appease a number of reviewers who tell him what to do, take too much of his time and get on his nerves. Eventually, a book for him is a way to write what he wants, the way he wants and be able to claim full credit for it. This might not be too far from reality for some if we think about the time needed to publish an article in a top journal. I have published some of my books, from contract to final editing in less than twelve months. How many articles take longer?

In terms of wording, an article and a book have a different structure. An article is shorter but often denser whereas in a book you take the time, and space, to develop and elaborate on more ideas. As a term of comparison, a book could be 80.000 words or even less. Think of a mini-book series that several commercial publishers have come up with to encourage authors to publish with them. I am talking of a text that is a bit longer than a wordy article, about 40.000 words.

Therefore, if you have 12 months free from any obligations, should you prepare a book or spend the equivalent time working on articles?

The value of a book, or an article, depends on the discipline you work in. In the social sciences and the humanities, a book still has a symbolic value. It is a way to enter academic adulthood and you might need it to be recognized as a scholar. In other disciplines, a book can be regarded as a waste of time, since you are mostly credited for articles. But there are some reference points you might want to take into account.

In some systems, a book is a formal requirement towards either tenure or a promotion. In other words, failure to produce a book at some point in your career might slow down your career progression.

In some other systems, there is a fixed number of points you can claim for each publication, but the points are not always proportionate to the effort. Think of a system that gives you one point per article and three points for a book. All the rest being equal, what is better for you then depends on how easily, and quickly, you can publish either. I am assuming here there are some scholars more at ease publishing articles and others better equipped to write books. If the peer review process for you is so painful and time-consuming that you really prefer writing 100.000 words instead of three articles, then go for a book. In other systems the ratio is five to one, that is a book that is worth five points and an article one. But I do not rule out that in some other systems a book and an article might have the same value for the national institution in charge of academic outputs.

In the end, you should choose your strategy after reading the guidelines for evaluation in the place where you want to progress in your career or apply for a fellowship. Once you are clear about what you want to achieve formally (get a promotion, have higher chances to be invited somewhere) you could look at the more informal effects of your publication. Generally, my question is: "How will the publication be received by the international academic community?" This is even more subjective, and personal, since it depends on how you want to position yourself within a discipline, a sub-discipline and thus how your colleagues (including potential enemies and competitors) will react to a book or to one article of yours.

Applied vs. fundamental research

Scientific research moves along a spectrum between fundamental and applied research. Fundamental research asks theoretical questions and attempts to solve problems regardless of their applicability in real life. It reflects on theoretical paradigms, sometimes with no real connection with the reality we live in. The underlying assumption is that results will be used by other researchers to solve a real-life problem at some stage. Applied research, in contrast, starts from a real-life problem being addressed. By doing so, however, it might also point out some deficiencies in general theory or suggest alternative theoretical paradigms that come to challenge existing ones.

In other words, fundamental research might explore what is the interaction between two organisms in a given environment (or just in a vacuum). Applied research will ask why two organisms, in a given geographical area, with some particular environmental conditions, have interacted in a way to generate, say, an epidemic and how this could be avoided, either in that given environment or in general.

Fundamental research in academia traditionally enjoys a relatively higher status than applied research. However, when research meets politics this tendency is reversed. A politician might want to be able to explain what problems science is solving with taxpayer's money and this answer, "Our scientists are thinking intensively about the questions: who are where and what is the meaning of life?" might not be sufficient. By the very nature of evidence-based policy, one needs to be able to use the sequence: we have a problem, so we invest in science to solve it. This has also led a number of politicians to attack, or at least criticize, disciplines that are regarded as detached from reality, not creating labor force or not generating economic opportunity for a country.

It is indeed difficult to explain sometimes that we are investing in something that we do not really understand now but we should bring some results in about ten or twenty years. Politicians need to be re-elected four or five years from now and they need to prove that their decisions positively impact the country. A promise that the country will benefit from something in ten years might not really work.

This has defined two distinct directions in academic approaches and support for research.

With some exceptions, whatever funding is awarded for research projects is intended to bring the first results during the course of the project (therefore, something should already be visible within four or five years, but sometimes in two or three). As a result, scholars working with external funding must be extremely short-term oriented and possibly apply their research towards some other issue that is perceived as more urgent and important by the donor, and possibly by the general public.

There is less pressure to do this, however, when research is funded through the general budget of a department or faculty. Researchers are allowed to think and the only obligation they have is to publish enough to justify the amount of money allocated for a university.

These two directions are, most of the time, combined. Indeed, research often has gaps between fundamental and applied research depending on a number of factors. One relatively recent tendency is to study a particular phenomenon within a discipline. Coventry University invested, some years ago, in "The Centre for Trust, Peace and Social Relations." Trust can be studied empirically, applied to a country or area, and theoretically, as a subtopic of several disciplines ranging from psychology to political science and economics.

In the end, donors are increasingly keener on applied research since the range of applicability about research is very broad. Even development agencies or government institutions might want to get endorsements from the researchers so to show to taxpayers, or critics, that the evidence used for their evidence-based interventions, has been collected in a scientific and systematic way. However, there are still several funding opportunities for researchers willing to concentrate on fundamental research.

It is useful to keep in mind this distinction to inform your own career strategy that should somehow solve the dichotomy between these two approaches. One is to start from a given theory to test it in a given environment, and inform theoretical journals, disciplinary conferences. The other is to start from a real-life situation to reflect on how things evolved in that particular way and, where appropriate, check if the explanation can help engaging with general theory on a given topic.

In the social sciences, for instance, there has been a relatively strong separation between area and disciplinary studies. Area studies researchers, journals and conferences, are interested in a particular world region and its development. As a result, an empirical study with little theoretical engagement might be interesting to a journal or an audience because, possibly based on newly generated data, it offers some explanations on why a given phenomenon has evolved in a given way in a given environment. Explanations could go as far as to engage with broader theoretical paradigms and even challenge a general theory. However, inasmuch as knowledge on a region or country is advanced, engagement with social theory is not necessarily expected. Disciplinary journals or conferences tend to appreciate works, including those based on empirical data collection, inasmuch as a study can locate in current debates and explain the significance of its findings not for a given context but for a broader audience.

As a journal interested in Southeast Asia I would be interested in a study on Vietnam because I am interested in the country. But if you try to send your article to a general social theory journal, whose readership spaces from scholars interested in the EU, or the US, to those interested in South America, your question should be, "Why is someone doing research on

Suriname when they should be interested in what I write on Vietnam?" An answer could be "because the article attempts to engage with general theory with regards to a particular issue." In the end, it is not so important how marginally, small or politically unimportant the area you study is. What is crucial is your capacity to capture audiences' interest in other regions or related phenomena who will find your article somehow useful for their own research.

Imagine a hypothetical situation, where a global publisher is trying to sell your book about funeral rituals in Albania across the globe. Departments dealing with Balkan studies will be likely to buy it. Perhaps departments where people doing similar research are based will also be interested. But why a general anthropology or sociology department should buy your book (that is most likely sold in hard copy at over €100) instead of something much more relevant to what their researchers are doing? Framing becomes then important and you have to make a choice.

Your book could:

Use your local findings to engage with general theory on rituals and then locate your results in social theory paradigms. In this case, you start from your empirics to engage with global debates and advance theory. The place where the data has been collected is not as important as the novel theoretical directions that it, and their interpretation, could point to.

Explain in detail funeral rituals in Albania, framing them in a historical and cultural context to try to become a reference for any further empirical studies on the topic and in the region. This would drive the book into the category of applied research and make it extremely valuable to anyone doing similar research on the region but not necessarily important to anyone beyond the region.

Is it worth paying publication fees? On the boundary between predatory and non-predatory journals

Publication (or submission) fees can be used by the journal for any one (or combination) of the goals below.

To reduce the amount of submissions that a journal receives: if you are the editor of the best journal in your field, you will certainly receive a fair amount of good quality articles. But how many scholars just send something thinking "one never knows." Some might genuinely think that they have an excellent article, some others simply overestimate their writing skills and do not devote enough time to writing and polishing. Whatever the reason, receiving extra articles is a cost for a journal. Even more when 80 percent of the papers you receive are not even worth sending out for peer review. This is the moment when you understand that you need an entry barrier. Asking perspective authors to pay a fee, at submission or upon acceptance, reduces the amounts of submission you will get. A possible drawback is that it also reduces the geographic distribution of potential authors since scholars from lower-income countries, and universities have lower available budgets for such activities.

To pay for editorial costs that are not paid by through any other means: in addition to reduce the number of submissions, and the amount of work you need to perform, submission or publication fees can also generate some extra income. If the budget of a commercial academic journals is limited, the budget of independent journals (managed by a department or an organization) is even more limited. Extra funds are always welcome and can pay for a variety of expenses or allow the journal to develop in a new direction.

To make money just as a company: I consider this aspect as defining the borderline between a predatory and non-predatory journal. Even when a company manages a journal and is eager to squeeze money out of public knowledge, the presence on the board of "allegedly" established academics guarantees a certain quality threshold below which the journal will not go. When this threshold is very low, or virtually inexistent, and the main approach is "the more we publish (no matter what quality), the more we make money," then the journal could be classified as predatory.

How to tell a predatory journal from a non-predatory one? I do not think there is a rule where to draw the line at. One could say that predatory journals solicit manuscripts, but also so may newly established journals. Sometimes, after participating in a conference, you might receive a message asking you to consider submitting your paper to a journal. In some cases, it is some new dubious journal that is looking to maximize the amount of submissions, and therefore income. In some other cases, it could be a decent journal targeting participants from a conference that is well known for attracting excellent papers. If the average quality of the papers at that conference is high, then soliciting articles from all of the participants could be a good strategy. After all, once the manuscripts have been submitted they still need to be accepted and the editor usually reserves the rights to reject a paper. No matter whether the paper was solicited or submitted spontaneously if its quality is inferior to the one expected by the journal it can still get rejected.

Between good and predatory journals there is a continuous line and many journals might fall in between these two categories. Whether you should be interested in a journal or not depends, ultimately, on your strategy and career goals. I usually ask myself the following questions:

1. What is the strategic importance of that article, and journal, to my career? Maybe, formally, that article has no impact on my career path. But, in contrast, I always wanted to write an article on a given topic and that outlet promised to publish it quickly. Or I need an article as a preparatory exercise for a better article to be submitted to a better journal.

2. How does the journal rank in my national ranking? Will I be able to claim any credits for an article published in that given journal?

3. If the article is published in that journal, will I be happy to advertise it or try to hide it, hoping that nobody will find out about that publication? Or will I just leave it as it is? That is, I will not make any efforts to advertise it since there is not much originality but, at the same time, I know that the article is decent and there is no need to hide it.

The answers to these questions are highly personal and subjective and can justify targeting journals that are regarded as "bad" in some national systems because they are considered decent in others. I am not encouraging you here to submit to predatory journals. For one thing, the boundary between journals, in terms of quality, is less clear than one might think. In general, each journal offers you some benefits at a given cost. Once you weigh the costs and benefits of a publication in a given journal, you can decide whether to go forward or not.

Open access vs commercial publishers

Publishing open access means to make your work accessible to the entirety of the academic community, or of the planet if you prefer. By contrast, when you publish with a commercial publisher, access to your work is restricted, to various extents, to only those who are willing to pay to read it. Note that there are several models of open access. The green one allows self-archive of the pre-print version of an article that becomes available for anyone through a given website. It maintains access restricted, however, the final version of the article is available only on the journal's website. By contrast, the gold one allows virtually anyone to download and read the article directly from the journal's website. This happens because either a fee has been paid or because the journal is non-commercial and allows free access to its articles. In the first case, in my view, we cannot really talk about open access. It is just that the authors bail out the article by paying for other people to view it, a bit like the old Neapolitan tradition of offering a coffee to people you do not know. In the second case, I usually am talking about open access.

With few exceptions, you receive no monetary compensation for an article. My logic would be that, inasmuch as you do not get more money by publishing with a commercial publisher, your preference should go to publications that make your work largely available. The problem with this reasoning is that the currency in the academic sector is prestige, a thing that is unevenly distributed across individuals and publishers.

As an emerging (and little known) academic, your goal is to gather readership, get recognized as a good researcher and become more visible. Most of the journals (or publishers) that offer you this perspective are managed by private companies whereas the number of journals that are open access and can offer you the same prestige (or a fraction of it) is limited, especially in some disciplines. As an established academic you could challenge this order. In principle, whatever you write and wherever will get published, people will read it and appreciate it. But an established academic wishing to break this vicious circle would be under pressure from other established academics who are not willing to challenge the current status quo. Besides, if publishing in the most prestigious journals becomes easier and easier, as your career progresses, what is your motivation for challenging the system and advocate for only open access publishers? Some people do it, but they are in the minority, and thus not sufficiently visible yet. Some others do it from time to time, alternating open and closed access publications.

What your strategy should be depends on the career level you are at and on your personal choice. Anyone starting their career should target prestigious journals that, with the exception of some disciplines like astrophysics, offer restricted (or gold upon payment of a fee) access to articles.

Going for a prestigious commercial publisher and have the money to pay for gold open access is probably the best choice, cynically speaking. Especially in disciplines where the best publishers are commercial, you get both glory and visibility. You also have a competitive advantage because many other authors, publishing in the same journal, might not have the money to pay for gold open access. However, this choice means to endorse the current system, where companies make money and academics with less money are penalized.

Second best choice still might be to publish in a journal with restricted access. Your article will still be visible to scholars and students from the richest (and possibly most important) universities. Limitations will apply towards re-using your article's content or republishing it but they might be worth the candle since, by publishing in some given outlets, you will be considered having reached the hall of fame of academia.

In a more down-to-earth perspective, an open-access article means that everyone, and especially academics and students from poorer universities, will be able to read your article. Someone with no electronic library access will start their search from documents freely available on the Internet, and yours will be there for them. Especially at the beginning of your career, you need some citations to boost your profile. With established academics busy citing one another, your marketing strategy could be to make your work available to the maximum amount of people so to increase the likelihood of it being cited.

There is also a midway solution. First, there are some emerging journals that, relatively established, try to maintain an open access status and thus would give you a combination of prestige and accessibility. Second, in many cases now it is possible to upload the pre-printed version of an article in your university's repository so to make your article with a prestigious commercial publisher widely available (usually called green access). Since it is not the final version, it is not as nice to look at, but at least you can share your work with whoever is interested in it.

The monopoly of prestige: more on commercial publishers

Journals managed by commercial publishers end up generating money for the company through subscriptions fees from databases and libraries. This is, in principle the long-term effect of an investment made many years ago and that brought in a good return. Even if you have a group of scholars that take care of the content, there are still a myriad of tasks to pay for and, in the pre-Internet and pre-laptop era, these tasks were extremely expensive.

At a time when copy-editing, typesetting, lay outing, printing and distributing cost quite some money, some entrepreneurial people proposed to take care of this process and to generate money to pay for their services by selling a final product to interested actors (libraries, then databases, individual subscribers).

As the academic market expanded, the business started becoming increasingly profitable. Besides, academics, trained to work for free, made themselves content with the prestige they could receive by publishing in a given journal or acting as chief editor for another. The situation, up to now, is win-win, at least in theory. Academics win prestige and companies make money. But they make money by asking authors to pass up their economic rights on their work (articles) and then restrict access to these articles to be able to sell them (single articles or journal issues) for a fee. In exchange, they offer support, at various degrees, throughout most of the editorial process, from submission to printing.

Seems like a fair deal. However, recent developments in academia made people question this model. First, some of them have started asking, "Why should knowledge (usually publicly generated, since most scientists are hired by public universities), and science be restricted in terms of people, and countries?" A solution has been proposed and commercial publishers have offered green and gold open access options. Upon payment of a fee, the article becomes freely accessible on the Internet and this might be an ideal option for an author. You get the prestige you were aiming for by publishing in that high-level journal and make your article readable by everyone.

Second, and equally important, the fee is compensating the company for the loss of not being able to sell your article, and allegedly cover their costs. But how fair is this model and what is the fee covering? In the Internet and laptop era, what is the cost of running a journal? If the editorial board works for free, reviewers work for free and you have no assistant willing to take up the copy-editing and layout tasks, how much would this cost?

Not much, in my experience. The journal in which I am a co-editor of is open access. It is not the most prestigious and famous in the world, but it can be classified as decent. Had we an editor more established than I am, I suspect we would attract even better, and more, articles. For the moment, however, we have a board, a peer review process and can offer articles of an acceptable quality, design and layout. We gave up the paper version some years ago to cut the budget and be more eco-friendly, but the result is that our annual budget, for two issues containing 8–10 articles and 2–4 book reviews is about the same as the money demanded by some commercial publisher to make one single article from the same discipline open access.

It could be argued that these companies provide a service, and this is the price of a service. If you want something different, or to pay a lower price, you can go elsewhere. True, but commercial publishers have a quasi-monopoly on a prestige market. Who can allow themselves to "go elsewhere" and get less prestige for a publication? Even established academics find it hard to challenge this monopoly, let alone anyone who feels unsure about their career. I could imagine a few people thinking "a last commercial publisher, then I go open access," (sounds a bit like "the last cigarette"). However, for most disciplines prestige is concentrated mainly in the hands of a handful of publishers, skillfully managed and that have an excellent advantageous position.

This is not to say that all journals that are in Scopus are managed by commercial publishers. A few of them are open access and some others may refer to other business models. The problem, in my view, is that academics often have been trained to think about the commercial model for publishing as the standard one and only sporadically can one meet groups of academics who try to challenge this view.

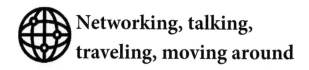 Networking, talking, traveling, moving around

Why should I attend a workshop instead of a conference, or a congress?

There are several settings in which academics present their work. Main ones are workshops, conferences and congresses are possibly the most common ones. Which one to choose to present your work depends on what stage you are in your research.

A workshop usually designates an environment in which only a limited number of participants are invited to somehow work together. As a result, you get to interact, at least potentially, with all of the other participants. There is no universally accepted format but, in general, only one session is held at a time, so you get the chance to attend them all. It could be open or closed to the public, but I would expect only a small turnout to attend and each presentation would be listened to carefully and critiqued. Feedback would be relatively detailed, so much so that a workshop is an ideal place where to present your work in progress, get engaged in discussions, network and get acquainted with a number of other scientists. With limited attendees, ideally, the organizers would manage to set up a few networking sessions, such as coffee breaks or informal dinners, which allows a chance for participants to get to know each other. You will get to know only a limited number of colleagues, but you can spend more time with them and deepen your knowledge of the ones that you find more interesting, useful or simply have the most in common with.

Conferences, and to a larger extent, congresses, face you with a different dynamic. The number of attendees may be higher, up to several thousand of them. There are several sessions happening at the same time and you need to give much more thought to decide where to go, what to attend, and with whom to network. Social interaction tends to be wider but shallower, chances are that you might not meet the same person twice. On the other hand, you will have access to hundreds of people that you might want to know. You will need to spend some time to study the program and find a way to meet the ones you find interesting, or simply want to get to know. By force of this, a session may be attended by a higher number of people than a workshop and many of them will not know you, and/or might be there just by coincidence or mistake. The main goal, when attending a conference, at least for me, is not to get feedback but to make your work visible to the maximum number of people. As a result, it might be worth it to use conferences as showrooms for your finalized work, presenting an already published paper or at least research that you have completed. People there need to know you through what you do, not what you plan to do.

How to choose the perfect event for you at a given stage in your career?

I distinguish conferences into two categories: regular or irregular. Irregular ones are organized whenever there is extra funding available in a research institution and they think it is worth investing into an international event. By force of this, you will see an announcement at some point on the Internet, but you cannot possibly predict in advance when it will happen.

Regular conferences are another story. You know well in advance when and where they will take place and they are usually organized by the same institution, usually a professional association, or at least by a university. The hardcore attendees are members of that association, or people with a long-standing relationship with the university, but you also have a substantial amount of newcomers. The scientific scope of the conference is usually wide and the title is sufficiently inclusive so that everyone can fit in, as long as they approach the topic from an angle that the association prioritizes.

Depending on the professional association, or associations, behind them, conferences will target a particular group. Disciplinary conferences will try to gather the maximum amount of people from a given discipline (e.g., sociology, biology, anthropology), either from a given region or worldwide. Thematic conferences will encourage participation by all scientists working on the same topic based in a given area (e.g., European Association for Cancer Research, American Association for Cancer Research) or worldwide. Regional conferences will target scholars working on a given region (e.g., Asian studies, Latin American studies) from a variety of disciplines as long as they are interested in the region.

Why is this distinction important? Because, to maximize your outcome, you should reflect on where you are going and what you can expect from a conference before applying for it. At any rate, it might be a good investment to attend at least one conference organized by one of your national associations. Even if you only work in English and most of your collaborations are international, your university is still funded nationally, and your national authorities rely on their pool of national scientists. Connections in your own country means the capacity to apply for national grants, to collaborate with national authorities and, eventually, be able to lobby or to unite forces with other colleagues to negotiate with the government. This is important in the case of, for instance, budget cuts. It is important that your colleagues from the same country know that you are there and active.

If you plan to look for a job on the American academic market, it makes little sense to apply for a European conference. Chances are that some American scientists will attend because they are working with some European counterparts, but the majority of the speakers will be from European research centers. If you are looking for a job as a sociologist, then a sociological association should be your starting point. Conferences organized around a region, or a topic, are tricky. You will definitely meet people interested in your area, or topic, and you will have something in common with most of the other participants, but there is no guarantee that you will meet the people who are key to landing you a job or in a circle that you want to be invited into. Eventually, experience and a "trial and error" approach will tell you where is the best to go but, meanwhile, you might want to check who is on the organizing committee, what are the main research centers involved and who is on the management board of the association to get an overview of what you might find once there.

Academic and professional associations: who needs membership?

When you apply for a job, or simply compile your CV for some database, you are often required to list the professional associations of which you are a member of. The range of associations, and memberships, available is almost endless. If we are talking about academic associations, I categorize them into three types:

- o Disciplinary (astrophysics, political sciences, anthropology, medicine, etc.)
- o Topical (promoting a multi-disciplinary perspective on a given issue or a sub-branch of a discipline, e.g., identity, conflict, cancer, and tropical medicine)
- o Regional (gathering those studying a particular area or region of the world)

The above foci could be combined and lead to further associations that occupy a particular niche like social scientists working in Central Asia or immunologists working in Southeast Asia.

However, even just a membership in some association may be preferable to non-membership. Being a member allows you to become involved at different levels within the association, at least potentially. Some of the possible benefits of being part of an association:

- o Receive information from the association mailing list (and can potentially post on it).
- o Attend the annual (or regular) event (usually a conference or a congress) organized by the association.
- o Present a paper at the regular event or at a minor one sponsored by the association.
- o Organize a panel at the regular event.
- o Serve in the organization committee for the regular event.
- o Organize some other minor events sponsored by the association. Often, between two regular conferences or congresses, the association sponsors some smaller events (e.g., inter-congress, workshops).
- o Serve as a member of the board for the association (including president or secretary general).

The bottom line is that you can pay for a membership (and become a member) if you just wish to attend the annual event organized by the association, or if you need to include in your CV that you are a member of some association. Often it is cheaper to pay for the membership and the event fee than paying for the event fee alone and this is done in order to increase the formal number of (non-necessarily active) members of an association. The rationale is that, the more members you have, the more you can show that your association is relevant to the academic community.

For many, being a member of a given association often implies that you sometimes attend some events and, thus, can potentially reach a given audience. It is an indicator of whom you are looking for in an audience, with whom do you seek dialogue and with whom you interact with. Associations have their mailing lists, groups, fast-track channels. They might interact with politicians, business partners or other stakeholders. Your potential employer will think of the benefits of having someone, in their team, member of this, or that, association depending on their own strategy. Some employers might want to hire someone who moves through the same associations current department members are already members of so to increase the presence of their research group, or a particular attitude, there. Some other employers might want to "use" their new staff to reach out to new audiences, a thing that is possible if you have people who are members of other associations.

In a best-case scenario, for your employer, membership of a given association means that you are an active part of a given community, an indicator through which channels you move, which debates, or approaches, you tend to engage with. In addition, because professional associations often have their own journal, it is also telling of which journals you might be reading or have access to, in case. If I have to choose a new colleague, or associate, I might be interested in seeing that they move through the same debates I move through or, in some cases, that they engage with other, possibly complementary, debates to be able to reach out to a wider audience.

In general, the more you are a member of, or active in, a variety of associations, the more you are likely to have more contacts than the standard person who has few or no memberships, in theory at least. It becomes then a question of what associations to join, at least strategically. As an anthropologist, your preferences could go to the American Anthropological Association, to the European Social Anthropological Association or to your national anthropological association or some more specialized ones such as the association of urban anthropologists, Southeast Asian anthropologists and so on.

One, two, or (too) many memberships? How many is too much?

Perhaps I am not the most relevant person to explain how to choose a professional organization since I am a polygamous nomad of associations. I mean that I have been a member of many but never followed one regularly or dogmatically. I have colleagues who, more faithfully, attend the same conference(s) every year or refer to the same association all the time. However, my experience might also inspire some to do the same, or to avoid my path.

My strategy has been to go where the wind took me. Sometimes a colleague invited me into a panel, some other times I just decide to test an association or an event. Obviously, I cannot attend all conferences and be involved as a member all the time. But one can alternate. A colleague I met at a conference said, "This is a fine one if you come once every other year, not every year."

In the end, I am not very active in any of the organizations I gravitate towards, but I converse with people from various disciplines, areas and spend a bit of time with this group of people and a bit with that one. The advantage is that I constantly broaden my view on things, I can see my own research from a variety of perspectives, get useful and less useful feedback from a variety of disciplines and I somehow "befriend everyone." The disadvantage, if I may call it so since I do not miss it, is that I am not progressing in status within any association. Nobody entrusts me with an important task or asks me to join a board or working group within the organization.

There is no best strategy but once a friend told me, and I agree, that people who become good at one thing reach success, or some kind of status, faster than people who invest into several things at the same time. But the latter, in the long run, are more likely to achieve more.

By the same token, I see two ideal-types of patterns of professional development, when it comes to membership and activeness in professional associations.

If you choose an association and start attending all of the meetings, chances are that you will end up mingling with the "right people." You will be asked to perform some tasks, help with organizing events, chair sections and will gain the trust of fellow members. You might eventually also move up to the board or be a part of the organizing committee for some larger events.

People within the association will come to know your name and at least get curious about what you are doing. Now, most associations have members based in several departments, and countries. Because the academic world is relatively small, chances are that within 4–5 years your name will sound familiar to a number of people, and departments, that are somehow related to the association.

But, once your professional life starts rotating around a particular association and you have a certain level of status there, why would you want to try something else? Why try and join another association that could give you a different perspective, and contacts within a different professional milieu, but where you would start from zero? It is still possible that you will be introduced to some key person from another association who already knows your work, so you do not really start from zero. But the general rule is that, if you feel too comfortable in a given environment, you tend to stay and have little incentives to explore the world beyond it.

A "nomadic" lifestyle, that is choosing to experience several conferences and test several associations without really finding a home, will allow you to explore several environments at the same time. But your interaction is likely to be less profound, or intense, than in the case where you invest yourself into one or two associations. You will find yourself often starting from the beginning at a conference, knowing only those who have invited you. You will also have to take part in a number of "graveyard panels" and start from zero again and again at each event.[19]

---

[19] A graveyard panel is a panel scheduled for the last day, or last session, of a conference, when most people are already gone. When you plan your conference, you want to make sure to sell your jewels well, so a keynote speaker is usually on the first or second day.

Chances are that you will eventually follow the pattern above and settle down with one or two associations. You will get there later than someone who has joined the association five years before but with some understanding of other associations and possibly more confident that this is what you want.

I see a strong analogy with the situation where you want to choose a partner. You can meet someone and think that you feel comfortable enough to commit for some years or you can go on and try several options for some time, before eventually making your choice. If you stop immediately you will have more time to build up and consolidate your relationship. At some point, you might ask yourself if the decision was too rushed, or how would you interact with different people. If you make your decision after trying a few partners, you will become more aware of what the alternatives are. Eventually, once you make your choice, you will start building a relationship "later," compared to those who have started a few years before you.

Making a decision about your position concerning a professional association is a strategic choice that you will have to deal with at some point in your career and it might be influenced by your desire to get a job in a particular place. If there is a university, or better a department, where you would like to work, try to figure out at what conferences, or around which journals, your potential colleagues tend to associate themselves with and try and join them. An informal conversation with a colleague from that department, at a conference dinner, sometimes is worth 1000 recommendation letters when you apply for a position.

Why organize a panel at a major conference?

In contrast to the amount of time, and effort, needed to just send an abstract to a conference, the work needed to pull together participants for a panel,

---

Likewise, the most popular topics, and academic stars, are to be put at the beginning. Eventually, those who do not fit the conference too well, who are not famous or whom you do not care about, will be scheduled for an anonymous panel on the last day that few, if any, will listen to.

coordinate them, respond to their queries and then manage a session is much more time-consuming. So, why not just submit something and let that someone else do it for you? After all, arranging papers into panels is a crucial task of conference organizers. Why bother? I have several reasons why I have come to prefer a panel to a paper.

First, a panel gives you a chance to invite people you have never had the chance to meet in person, or just to entice some of your best colleagues and friends to present with you. It also increases your chances of being accepted because, eventually, a panel is a finished product. As the organizer, if I have one paper on a specific topic for the whole conference, I might not know where to insert it and, by force of this, I might have to reject it. The intrinsic message of a panel is "We are a team already. Just give us 1,5 hours somewhere and you will not have to deal with our papers or find a place for them."

Organizing a panel gives you an extra chance to end up with people who are doing similar things as you. Not all organizers have the time, desire, or capacity to find a panel matching your paper. Sometimes there are not enough abstracts on your topic, but the organizers might want to accept you anyway for many reasons. Or else, not enough people sent an abstract or they have a target in terms of how many conference fees they need to collect to fund the conference. Perhaps the selection committee likes your abstract or would like you to attend and, only when the selection is complete, they realize that there is not a panel that really fits your topic. Whatever the reason, this might mean that your paper on religion in Serbia ends up in a panel on Brazilian ecology.

A panel is your chance to decide whom you are going with to a given conference and whom to debate with. It is also a chance to invite more senior scholars to join you and take advantage of their audience, who will come to listen to your colleagues but will stay for your presentation. If I have a particular public in mind for my presentation and I know that inviting someone will bring it to my panel, I will try to invite that person. I do not mind doing some extra administrative work as long as this brings me extra visibility.

Other advantages of contributing to a panel, or an event

Many special issue journals, or edited books, are drawn from successful conference panels. Now, pulling together a panel with 3–4 more presentations will not enable you to publish an edited collection after it. But the papers you have in your panel could be the initial core part of a book, or a special issue, that you can fill in with a call for papers later on. Alternatively, you could use the papers from your panel to propose a journal symposium, for which four papers are enough.

A panel is also a way to become visible to a wider audience and show that you are active, have international contacts and get things done. Think of the case where you need an expert on a given topic and do not know where to look for one. A good place to start could be to check who has organized an event, or at least a panel, on a similar issue. I once needed a partner from Latvia for a project and did not know anyone. There are many university professors I could write to. In principle, I could simply spam anyone working on that topic, broadly defined, and see who would answer. However, apart from being time-consuming, how would I know if that person is not only interested in my project but also capable of managing some tasks? I came across a panel organized by a Latvian professor and my assumption was if she had taken responsibility for something and was managing a panel, she was somehow administratively capable and able to manage some tasks. I wrote to her, she replied, and we started working together.

On another occasion, a colleague asked me to find a few organizations, and individuals, from the South Caucasus region, that would participate in a Volkswagen-funded project. I had some contacts but not enough to build a network and there was little time. In addition, I wanted to reach out to people outside my friend's friends. I knew about a Swiss-funded academic network that had prized a few scholars from the region. I checked the network's website and wrote to all the award winners. My assumption was that, if a researcher has been awarded some research money they must have written a good project and, if they were also managing it, they must have some administrative experience.

You can still try to involve someone you have met at a conference into a project, but you cannot be as sure of their administrative skills as you can be with someone who, you know, is actually managing a project. A panel is a mini project, it can be organized with little effort and by people who are administratively messy, but it is a milestone and, between a scholar who has never organized a panel and one who has, I would always choose the latter.

Will your university care that you are organizing a panel? Not always or necessarily, but when you apply for a job, in some places they ask what kind of international events you have organized. If you have never organized a real conference, you can still claim that lack of money was the main reason, but you have pulled together a panel at a conference. One could thus reasonably assume that, giving you some money, you would find the time and capacity to organize something larger than a panel. In the end, it is also about your own growth. Some people might feel confident enough to organize a whole conference at the beginning of their career, some others might not, and a panel is a way to dip your toes into the sea before going swimming.

Paper presenter, chair or discussant

I have never attended a conference without presenting anything, but it seems that some people do. Consider attending without presenting if you think you want to meet people from a given environment, but do not have anything ready yet (and have the money to go). But keep in mind that, with no presentation, you might look a bit less interesting (professionally speaking) than you would look with a presentation.

If attendance with no presentation is an option, hyperactivity throughout the conference is another one. You could attend and present your work in one or several panels. At some conferences, you are allowed to give more than one paper, so you could present at several panels. Some conferences only allow you to act as a presenter once, but you can still act as a chair or discussant in other panels.

Why should you bother yourself with extra work if you already have enough to do? Well, it is some extra work and it might be stressful, especially if you act as a discussant, but it brings you a number of advantages that it is worth at least considering. As a discussant, you will probably have to read the presentations that you will (hopefully) receive beforehand and then comment. It could be time-consuming—think of the case where you have to comment on four 20-page papers or, even worse, when the feedback is expected in written form. But this might be your chance to engage the speakers in a discussion. You could have a chance to promote your work, for instance, if some of the presentations relate to what you are doing. If presenters feel that some time has been devoted to reading their papers, and this has led to fruitful discussion, they will be pleased and will be happy to talk to you afterwards. This is especially useful if you are a young or emerging scholar and need to get noticed or to network as much as possible.

As a chair, you might have less intellectual interaction with the presenters, but you still communicate with them. It is your chance to do a good job and excel in good presentation or entertainment skills, or simply because you can keep time and demonstrate the authority to deal with a situation. But being a chair is interactive. If you happen to be in a panel where you can interact with your gurus, then they have to respect you, they have to speak to you. At the end of the session, you can also "abuse"—as some chairs say— your position as a chair and get to ask the first question together with, or after, the discussant.

Chair and discussant across cultures and scholar traditions

My understanding of a chair is very basic. You are there to introduce each paper, to ensure that speakers do not exceed the agreed time when delivering a presentation, and to moderate a discussion on the papers.

The discussant, when appointed, is in charge of commenting on the papers and asks the first questions in order to warm up a discussion, that will then be continued by the rest of the public.

Inasmuch as this sounds simple, there are so many cultural variables, and variations, that one should at least be aware that a "chair" or a "discussant" means many things depending on the context. It should be noticed that, although I speak of chair and discussant as two separate roles, at some conferences these two are merged into the single figure of the chair, who is in charge of both functions.

The way the discussant engages with the presentations can range from oral feedback on each of the papers to one simple question per presentation or to a written feedback in the form of an academic paper. Feedback could be elaborated to the point of being almost an oral peer review of the paper or simply some formal suggestions or requests for clarification. As a discussant, you might receive the presentations in advance, in the most diverse format (from PowerPoints to academic papers to a one-page outline) and with the most diverse timing. Some will send their presentations and fairly assume that you have read it. However, some others will still expect that you have read their 20 page papers even if it was sent an hour before the presentation. This is a very interesting phenomenon that I name "once it is clear in my mind then it exists, and it is thus clear to the rest of the world," like there was little or no gap between when the paper is in your inbox and when it is (digested and ready to discuss) in your mind.

As a chair, I believe that my task is to let the panelists shine so I take as little time as possible to promote myself. I introduce the presentations assuming that the presenters are the most competent people to explain what their paper is about and if they have something to share, they can do it without my help. I have happened to be, however, in an awkward situation where I was almost attacked for not reading out the long biography that each of the panelists had provided. Because these biographies were on the program, I assumed that anyone interested could just read them. I should thus not waste precious time by simply reading out what everybody could read by themselves. But, it seems, I was a victim of some cultural misunderstanding as I was supposed to share, clear and loud, all the achievements of each of the panelists. Going even further, I could also imagine a chair praising not only the panelists but also the papers and adding comments at some point in the paper.

In addition, a chair is faced with a classic dilemma in a panel: do we take questions after each of the presentations or do we collect them once all of the presentations have been delivered? Questions after each presentation would be fairer. Each presenter gets their share and questions come when the paper is still fresh in the audience's mind. By contrast, collecting questions at the end of the panel might mean more attention to the last paper, which is fresher than the first one in the public's mind. However, questions after each paper carry the additional risk of getting stuck on some discussion that gets out of control at some point and even reduces the time allocated for the last one or two presentations. I have seen many times an excellent timing for the first one or two papers, followed by animated discussions. Because they were too passionate and interesting to be interrupted, they left the last presenter not only a little time for questions but even for their presentation. Being this a very frustrating thing, especially for the presenter, my choice is always to let everyone speak the same amount of time and then leave time for a general discussion.

Finally, a chair should have the authority to stop the presentation when this goes on for too long. But this is only theoretical. What happens if the chair is a PhD student and the presenter to be stopped is the leading figure in a given discipline? Or in any hypothetical situation where the speaker is much more important than the chair? Will the chair feel confident enough to tell their line manager, advisor, academic director or simply to the leading figure of the discipline in their country "You have spoken enough?" This ultimately depends on the power relationship between scholars in a given context, but I have seen many cases where a speaker talks too much, and the chair is too embarrassed to bring it to their attention.

Publishing your work presented at a conference: is it worth it?

At events that I have organized I often get asked the question of whether the proceedings will be published or, at least, will the event result into any publication. It is certainly wishful thinking that you go somewhere, deliver a presentation and then with little or no effort your paper is published. Indeed, a colleague recently told me that her university funds participation in conferences only happen if a paper also results from it. I understand the logic: you (a university) are happy to invest into something that will increase your research output (measured by written publications). However, if you think that the most important conferences in the world do not necessarily guarantee publication then this strategy can be regarded as short-sighted. It basically discourages participation in some of the most important conferences in the world. By contrast, it encourages participation in mid or low range conferences that promise to publish some sort of proceedings of dubious quality. At any rate, you could at least get back to your line manager and claim an extra publication (possibly in English), a thing that in some environments still gets you some credit.

At large conferences, publication—as a direct outcome of a presentation—depends on individual initiative (i.e., a panel organizer who proposes to publish the papers presented in a section; an editor that you meet by chance at a wine reception) but there is not necessarily a central, or centralized, mechanism to publish papers. There are some exceptions, of course. I know of cases where large portions of the presentations have been published in some sort of Scopus-indexed collection, which makes both the presenter and the sending university happy.

Smaller workshops might follow different dynamics. They might even have been funded by a donor with the understanding that a publication will arise so that you are not only expected to contribute something but are actually requested to do so. Should you?

The spectrum of possibilities is large. Post-conference presentations may range from a 2-page text in an anonymous book collecting all the abstracts (or extended abstracts) to an e-book collecting all the presentations. It could also result into a book that becomes then somehow indexed into an international database.

Most important, and interesting, are the opportunities related to your individual network efforts. When I was still a PhD student I ended up by chance at a conference where one of the organizers had just been invited to prepare a special issue of a top journal. She liked my material and coached me from my presentation to submission of a paper that was then published in that journal. Since then, this has happened several times to me I jumped in immediately. When you are offered to contribute to a special issue of a Q1 journal you do not ask, just submit it and then ask.

But I have also been asked to submit papers that would then go into some semi-anonymous books and I have felt obliged to deliver something. In some cases, I have just adapted something that I had already written before, in other cases I have taken a chance and written down some raw ideas that one would not find room for in a journal article.

Why was I doing that? Several explanations about why I was doing that are possible. In general, I see this as a result of:

1. my academic ego—someone tells you that they will publish whatever you send them and, as an academic, I am dying to add another line to my list of publications. This is especially exotic if the publication is in a language I do not usually write in
2. some sort of moral obligation that I feel when someone invites me somewhere and pays for my travel. If I accept to be invited and know that they expect something, then I will not say that I do not have time for it. This could also be because I hope for some sort of visibility or at least to have evidence that I was part of a certain elite group or because I was treated well by very hospitable organizers.

I was recently invited to a NATO-funded conference that resulted into an edited book. I was happy to be able to write a chapter based on whatever was on my mind at that time but also expected that being involved in a book sponsored by NATO-funding could be seen as evidence that I was invited somewhere important.

If I have to systematize my choice on whether, or not, to send a paper after a conference that I have attended, this would be my strategic matrix:

Offer	Publication in conference proceedings	Chapter in a book with a minor publisher	Chapter in a book with a major publisher	An article in a journal's special issue
Attitude	Send something if you can spend 20–30 minutes maximum on it (something old but relatively unpublished)	Send something if interested in the exercise of writing or in publishing with particular people (or editors) or you want to be invited again	Send something if interested in the exercise of writing or in publishing with particular people (or editors). Or if in your national evaluation system this counts as academic output	Consider sending something if the journal is in a database that your academic evaluation system values

Something worth considering for all of the possibilities above, and in general participation in any collective project, is that it is always worth checking the management skills of the perspective editors. While the perspective of a (good) publication is certainly attractive, there are many cases where: a) the process is interrupted half-way or the publication takes years to see the light or, worse, b) the editors are so disorganized or pedantic that you end up working three times more than if you had submitted an article to a standard issue of a journal.

Presentation skills

I am writing this section while watching what I consider to be the academic equivalent of a horror movie. Someone is trying to fit a whole academic paper in a 15-minute presentation, which is already hard, while reading the paper aloud.

What should be my motivation to listen to this person? I can read their paper myself. If I go to a presentation it is to enjoy it, to get a summary of the main points in words other than the ones in the paper. Besides, by concentrating on reading the text the person is losing all their body language, intonation and emphasis that you can put into a presentation to interest your audience. In these conditions, a presentation becomes a monotone rush to be able to stuff in the maximum amount of words possible. It is not just about being able to deliver a presentation within the given time frame. A presentation is about fascinating your audience, convincing them that your paper, or yourself, are worth their attention more than the rest of the papers out there.

I appreciate the fact that people have different skills, and not everyone is a good presenter. But academics find themselves in the role of a public speaker quite often. Why not try to improve it? There will always be someone who, without many efforts, is able to run faster than you do but, with some training, you can learn to run faster than before. By the same token, there will always be someone better than you at fascinating audiences. But you do not need to be better than them, you just need to develop yourself to reach a higher, or at least acceptable, level.

There are trainings, courses, and guides on how to become a better public speaker, a convincing speaker and so on. I am not sure if all of this is needed when you just need to present some academic results. I do believe that academic presentations should be distinguished from business or marketing ones. However, in the end, a few small details can help you to better interact with the audience and make them feel more comfortable. You just need to pay attention to them and it might be sufficient just to record and then watch yourself to notice a few shortcomings of your presentation. Or take acting classes. If that has always been your secret dream, you could motivate your decision as professional development.

In the end, you might want to spend some extra time to fine-tune the following, in a presentation:

Body language: it is simply distracting, but in some cases also unpleasant, to look at someone who is scratching their head or body the whole time while speaking.

Intonation: not all the words you say have the same importance. You can accompany more important statements, or keywords, with changing the tone of your voice.

Speed: speaking faster to be able to use more words will probably decrease the quality of your message. Sometimes even a pause in the speech might be useful, inasmuch as it allows you to put extra emphasis on a concept, to create some sort of suspense.

PowerPoint: what people see on the wall should be distinguished from what you have in your notes. A PowerPoint presentation is intended to complement, or integrate, what you are saying, not to make your notes visible and read from them. The shorter the message on a slide the better, even more. If the slide contains visual material or just bullet points, your presentation will then be elaborated on orally.

In a presentation you are giving a sense of the paper, a pre-taste for people to get interested and eventually read your paper (or, at least, to cite its main message). In other words, you are marketing your paper and yourself. The clearer the message the more people will become interested. Not everyone has the same patience or concentration capacity. I am sure that even the worst presentation ever might still get some good feedback because someone in the audience was determined to follow it to the end, no matter how chaotic it was. What I am talking about here is speaking to an audience, not to the survivors of an audience. A succinct, short but dense message, with only a part of the paper explained, might work better than a long one that ticks all the boxes.

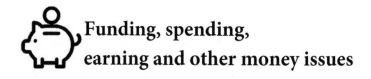 Funding, spending,
earning and other money issues

What makes a good fundraiser (in academia as elsewhere)?

The main criteria to identify a good fundraiser would be two, in my view: one is how many successful applications the person gets; the other is the total amount of money received over a given period. Think of the situation where, in a given year, fundraiser A receives 10 grants worth €10.000 each and fundraiser B receives 1 grant worth €100.000. Fundraiser A brings you the advantage of regularly applying for funding and good chances of receiving it. Fundraiser B is perhaps more irregular but spends less time writing grant applications to get you the same amount of money. I labor under the assumption that the administrative component of a grant application of €10.000 or €100.000 is not too big. The advantage of applying for a €10.000 grant is possibly that might have fewer competitors and higher chances of success.

I would keep in mind two principles when raising funds.

First, the money you get should allow you to do what you want, and what you need. If you win €5.000 every 4–5 years but this is sufficient to get what you want, and your line manager is happy with your work, then why should you bother applying for several million? Do it if you feel this is what you need, not because you have to.

Second, success in fundraising does not depend necessarily on how well you write, or how competitive your application is. Obviously, if you prepare a horrible bid, you are unlikely to convince any donors to give you money. But, and this is equally important, your success depends on the number of applications assessed better than yours.

I know of extremely competitive grants, where your chances would be close to zero to win. But I am also familiar with grants for several hundred thousand that have been awarded not to the best but to the only applicant(s). You will never know in advance how many people will apply for a given grant. Figures can change dramatically and applications in a given scheme drop to half or less in the space of one year. I have seen funding schemes with a success rate of 90% in a given year. I have also seen applications scoring 95/100 being rejected. But then the next year 85/100 would be enough to be awarded funding.

A good fundraiser is not good because they win all the time or write the best bids (what is the best bid anyway?). Good fundraisers create their own luck by being in the right place at the right time. You cannot control fate. But you can attempt forecasts, calculations and learn to sense where to apply for money. You can check statistics, success rates, and/or ask colleagues. But the way you need to write an application, and the chances for success you will have, depends also on whom you are competing with. Are you the most junior, or senior, of the applicants in the pool? Are you competing with scholars from the same discipline or from all disciplines? How large is the grant? Is it an individual or a collective research project? Do other applicants have the power to lobby the donor whilst you have not? Are the other applicants supported by external consultants or teams?

Why are some grants harder than others to get?

What determines competition for research grants? You can certainly learn to excel in your task, acquire further presentation skills, project management tools and write an excellent bid. But the higher you go the harder it gets. At the national level, you compete with the best domestic universities. At the international level, you might have to compete with the best universities in the world. The bigger a university is, the more money they have to invest in external consultants and employee training and development programs for their staff. No matter how well you write, there will always be someone who writes "better" than you and whose application will score better than yours. Your goal is, thus, not to write the best application but one that falls within the number of applications that will be funded.

The primary goal of a donor is to give out the money they have. The best projects they can fund the better. However, when a donor has more money than applicants a choice is needed. To grant funds to whoever is there or to cancel the competition? This decision depends on how free the donor is in their choices but keep in mind that budget projections for future years are made on the basis of what was spent in a year. If you underspend your budget, chances are that the following year you will get less money than this year.

This, at least to me, means that what determines the chances of success you have is not only how you write an application but also whom you are competing with and how many other applications the donor gets. If the donor has ten grants to award and your proposal is average, they will probably fund it if there are only nine more applicants. The alternative would be not to award enough money this year and they could eventually be blamed for not advertising their grant sufficiently or not doing something sufficiently relevant for getting attention.

When you were at school there was always a teacher that terrorized everyone, gave the lowest marks and everybody was afraid that they would not pass. Well, that was a risky business for the teacher. Eventually, a school teacher that has a failure rate of fifty percent can easily be considered a bad teacher. They do not explain things clearly enough, fail to take into account their pupils' necessities or simply chooses tests that are too difficult for the level they have in their class. Likewise, a donor that rejects all grants applications is a bad donor. This is why, in some cases, a donor might want to accept some weaker bids for the sake of meeting their target.

Your chances of success are directly linked with the number of applications a donor gets for a given scheme. The higher the number, the more likely that top universities and excellent scholars apply, the harder it is to get a grant. Now, how many applications a donor will get, and the average quality of the applications depend on two main things: how attractive is the package they offer for the Principal Investigator (PI) and how generous they are with overheads.

What grants are easier to get? Tip 1: look at the overheads

Overheads are a budget line in a grant that is not intended to cover the direct costs related to the implementation of the action or intervention. They are usually calculated as a percentage of the total amount awarded and the winner can dispose of it unrestrictedly. Overheads are intended as a contribution to the institution's general expenses (i.e., electricity, use of building) for managing the grant for the duration of the implementation of the project.

They can, for instance, be counted towards building rentals, telephone or Internet but also towards the working hours of people not directly hired through the grant. This is done because it would be difficult, or simply not worth it, to calculate the costs to a given university in terms of computer usage, use of offices, working hours of a financial administrator, how many bites of Internet traffic has been used. To cut things short, donors offer a percentage of the amount allocated for direct costs to cover some of the expenses incurred during the grant. This could go from as little as 0% to 100% in some exceptional cases. We are talking here about an amount of money that is not restricted, not auditable by the donor[20] and can be spent on anything. This includes the option of using this money to cover a deficit from another department, or faculty, as long as it is spent in line with national rules. In other words, it is a present, or a donation, to the university that can be used to cover any costs, including those not related to the grant.

Everyone wants more money and universities are not an exception. But what are you ready to "pay" to get more money? Generally speaking, a university is interested in investing money (or staff time) to win a bid if:

o They have a pre-defined annual budget to pay external consultants to prepare bids for the university.

o They are in countries with national funding allowing to hire external consultants.

o They have a tradition of applying for external grants and, when hiring a new staff member, they will give priority to a scholar with an excellent fundraising track-record.

o They are under pressure to secure external funding for a number of reasons. One of these could be prestige (or decreased funding from other sources such as regular funding coming from the state). Accordingly, they put a lot of pressure on their staff to write grant applications as often as possible.

The list is not exhaustive and there are scholars with good funding records, who play the game well, in minor universities. But if you look at the list of

---

[20] Your home institution, private or public, probably has to undergo a national audit once a year so you still have to ensure that you spend this money according to your national rule. The difference is that you can use it for costs that are not eligible by donor's rules since no audit will be performed by the donor on that particular amount of money.

grant awards, at least for EU-funded projects, you might notice a correlation between the level of prestige (and size) of universities being awarded the certain grants and the amounts of overheads included in that grant.

This is not to say that you should give up competing for large grants unless you are at a top university. Just be aware, the higher the level of overheads coming from a given funding scheme, the more likely major universities will apply for it, the higher will be the level of the bids and the stiffer the competition.

An opposite tendency can be remarked for grants that offer little or no overheads, or that even require some amount of co-funding. Major universities will rarely be among those winning grants where you have to contribute a share (10–20%) of your own money. Winners of these grants will usually be minor universities for whom securing external funding is already a success. They are under pressure to show to be competitive in international competitions. It means little to them that winning comes with strings attached and they will be happy to co-fund the grant as long as this allows them to rise in national or international rankings. After all, performing better at the national level might mean to receive a higher amount of funding from the state.

What grants are easier to get?
Tip 2: look at PI compensation packages

The other indicator of whom you will have to compete with for a grant is the package offered to the PI upon being awarded the grant. Salaries across Europe, and in general across the world, differ quite a lot. It could be fairly assumed that the more successful an academic is, the higher their salary is. It could also be assumed that the more a scholar is under pressure (to find permanent employment or to consolidate their position in a department) the more they will apply for external funding.

But few people are happy to apply for a grant that, if awarded, would give them a salary lower than the one they have at the moment. I would also assume that, the more you advance in your career, and thus your position in your department strengthens, the less you need to prove yourself by securing external money.

This determines a hierarchy in applicants for a research grant, especially one that is centered around a single scholar. In addition to the "overhead rule," the most successful academics would go for funding schemes granting them:

More money. Money is a motivator only if you do not earn enough, but this varies across countries and disciplines. If your salary level is already high, some additional money is barely a motivator. After all, we are in the public sector and there is a limit to how much your salary can be increased upon award. But more money will attract, in addition to anyone in an unstable position, the best academics of countries where salaries are low. There are sometimes superstars working in a country with low academic salaries who are regularly, not to say constantly, on some kind of external fellowship or grant.

Prestige. Some funding schemes, especially if associated with some prestigious donors, grant you extra prestige or access to further benefits. Think of chairs sponsored by world-known organizations or foundations. Even if they bring no money, they give you the chance to brand yourself. In a long-term, and strategic, perspective, this could be just the first step to advance in your career (i.e., ask for a promotion faster). You could also then apply for something more prestigious using the brand you just earned. Some academics earn enough not to care about additional money. But they might be motivated by the desire to secure themselves within the department. I am thinking about UK academics that have, in some cases, funding targets. I once heard a friend admitting that his department expected him to raise around €7M in the next six-year period to maintain his status. Not meeting this target would mean at minimum a damaging relationship with the management board, to say the least.

There is also the case of established academics from countries that do not provide enough additional research funding. They might need to buy an expensive piece of equipment or give employment to people they want to work with, or simply believe that their research will bring them glory and/or genuinely benefit the society.

Freedom. If your position entails lots of teaching, or administrative responsibility, bringing in external money might be a way to relieve you of your workload. In the English-speaking world one talks of bailouts. You take a leave and pay your salary from external funds, with your funds being used by the university to pay someone to temporarily teach in your place. After the project is over you get reintegrated into your department. In the case of an ERC grant that lasts five years, for instance, you might get relieved from teaching for five years, which is a long sabbatical leave in academia. Other universities, or countries, do not always institutionalize this practice. But you have definitely more leverage to ask not to do what you do not like if you are bringing in external money to a department.

Funding schemes that offer one, or more, of these elements, are more likely to be targeted by established academics. The lower you go on the scale, the less likely it will be that you will have to compete with the sacred monsters of academia, in your country as internationally. An anonymous foundation granting you €1000 for a project might not be worth the effort of preparing the documents. Nonetheless, if you are under pressure to win anything to show that you are active in fundraising, this could be your ideal choice since it should not be too hard to get. Those under high work pressure will think several times before applying for such minor grants since there is still some administrative work to complete, no matter how small a grant is.

So what criteria does one use when applying for grants? (seeing like a donor)

A friend was looking for a grant and I suggested that he apply for a funding scheme. Having never worked with him, I could not be sure of the quality of his application. But I had some strategic information suggesting that he had high chances. Early in the year, for other reasons, I had to study the website of a donor offering grants to scholars from the Southern Caucasus (Armenia and Georgia primarily). I had noticed, at that time, that funding was allocated primarily for Armenia and Georgia. However, for some reason, funding was going mostly to Georgia.

I suggested he apply for that grant scheme and he won. My reasoning had been that applications from Armenia would have more chances to be successful for two reasons. First, if few Armenians were winning this was, most likely, because the average quality of applicants from Armenia was lower than their Georgian counterpart. Second, a donor intended to fund Armenia and Georgia but funding mostly Georgia does not look good on paper. I figured that they would be more welcoming towards an additional Armenian application than a Georgian one. If the foundation had to show an impact in each target country and Armenia was lagging behind, their priority at that stage was to increase the number of grants going to Armenian organizations.

This logic does not always apply, sometimes geographical distribution is not so important. But the moral of the story is that it pays to reflect not only on what the donor wants you to deliver but also on what the donor is expected to deliver. Everyone has someone above them. Once you get funding, you are responsible before the donor is. But the donor also gets its money from somewhere (private donations, tax money) and has to promise to spend it in a way that is consistent with what they have stated when they got the money. In the case above, the goal was working towards capacity building of the Southern Caucasus academic institutions. For technical reasons, they had not included Azerbaijan. But then they were even keener to keep geographical balance and show that the money was at least going to the other two countries. This is the case of programs targeting a given region, where geographical spread is as important as scientific excellence.

In some cases, however, the donor is under pressure to demonstrate to be funding only the best of the best, with no disciplinary or geographical balance to be respected. If so, they could easily give several, or all, grants to institutions from the same country, disciplines or, in more extreme cases, to the same institution. In some cases, competitions are not even diversified across disciplines and you have philosophers competing with medical doctors with very little chances for the former to succeed. There are several reasons why I assume that, with a project equally well written, philosophers (and in general human and social scientists) have a weaker position than scholars from the hard sciences. First, if we take the section "impact of the research on society" it is more likely that applied research in medicine, biology, Information and Communication Technologies (ICT) has a more immediate, and visible, impact on society at large than its social and human sciences counterparts. Second, if there is a section on scientific merits of the PI or the team, people in the hard sciences are more likely to have more publications, citations and collaborations than people in the humanities and social sciences.

As a donor, you need to be able to defend your choices and prove, if asked, that your money is going to projects which will bring significant change in society. One way to assess the quality of the PI in a project is to measure the amount of citations they have attracted so far. As a result, it might become easier to justify a grant to someone who has a strong citation record. In the case of a mixed panel, that is when any scientist can apply regardless of their discipline, applicants from hard sciences disciplines have better citation records than applicants from the social sciences. This means that a junior scholar from biology, with relatively few citations, compared with others in their field, might have a much better citation level than some of the most established anthropologists who applied for the same grant. If no adjusting mechanism is foreseen, hard scientists will, on average, perform much better than social scientists for that any interdisciplinary or mixed funding scheme.

They say there is no money in academia, is it really so?

When you publish a journal article with a commercial publisher you are usually required to sign a copyright agreement. It is all too easy, and it now can be done online. It formally protects you from improper use of your material, which is a good thing. What you might fail to notice, however, is that the permission gives the publisher full economic rights on your work (on which you retain the moral rights, however). This means that there are limitations even for you to republish your own work.

A colleague wanted to reprint an article of mine and planned to pay for the translation. We went to the publisher to ask for permission to translate and print it. They said that permission would be granted but we would have to pay €500 for copyright clearance, that is to grant permission to reprint the article in Polish. I had no time to write a chapter for a book that I was editing so I considered reprinting a journal article I had just published. Clearance became a very complicated process, to the point that it became easier for me to rewrite the article than asking for permission.

After the episodes above, I started learning my rights and it turned out that I could reprint my articles for free only if they would go into a monograph that I was authoring or into a book that I was editing. At some point of my career, to tick the boxes for a professorship I needed to publish a monograph. I had no time, or desire, to do that at that stage of my career but, I thought, I could just demand permission and republish "the best of Abel" into a monograph. After all, I had the right to republish all my articles as long as they went into my own book. I went to ask for permission and got another surprise. I could reprint the articles published with a given publisher only if they would not make up more than 20% of the whole monograph. In other words, in a five chapter monograph, I would not be able to reprint more than one article from a given publisher. The rest could be reprinted but for a fee.

As a friend says, "Academic journals are the best form of exploitation: you have people who work for free and who are dying to pass their copyright to a commercial publisher that will then make money on their labor."

What is also interesting is that many academic publishers now work with a scaling down model that requires a book to come out first in hardcover at over €100. One of my last books was 182 pages and sold at €160. Basically, my book sold at the price of gold. If the book sells well, after a couple of years, the paperback will be issued at €25–30.

With these figures in mind, I find it quite surprising when I meet a colleague moaning that there is no money in academia. Or when someone offers 80 instead of €100 for a coffee break under the pretext that there is little money to be had. If you do not know it, find out what the budget in your department is. Then ask why in some cases finding €500 seems so difficult. You can also compare salaries across disciplines, junior and senior level, or between researchers and administrators. You might discover several interesting idiosyncrasies of the sector and discover that the money is there but in the hands of a few gatekeepers and it is often not evenly distributed. Some units have more money than they can spend but do not want to acknowledge it, or their budgets will be cut. Some other units might not have enough or be unwilling to spend on certain items. This can also depend on the decision-makers, managers and key persons of a given department who have a more, or less, conservative attitude. Your homework, if you want to have access to money, is to discover where it is available and then go for it.

So who are the gatekeepers of money (and power) in academia (and around academia)?

Some years ago, sometimes with some friends and sometimes alone, I started wondering if the current model of career growth in academia suited me. Of course, it did not but, by the time you are consolidated enough to do something about it, you are also to the point that you are losing your motivation to do anything about it.

You dream of a world where books are accessible, where connections are less important than quality, where "quality triumphs over evil." You do it in a mix of idealism and stress from your line manager who is asking you to learn to survive academia and deliver your outputs the way others, more senior academics, do. You do not know where to start to fight the system, so you just go the same way everyone is going (with the exception of some hardcore people who have all my respect and admiration) and, after a good deal of efforts, you learn the rules of the game. At some point, you find yourself in the condition of pleasing your line manager, and your national quality-control institution, very easily. You publish enough books and journals, mostly with commercial publishers selling at €120 per copy. But it takes relatively little effort for you to do that and you know that, once you have "reached your quota" with regards to the number of publications, you can then do whatever else you want, be this spending time with your family (is there anyone in academia really doing this?) or writing things that bring you no credit but pure pleasure.

Initially, it is hard to establish contacts with a publisher. I remember one response I got, "The idea is good, but we do not trust your ability, as junior scholars, to bring this edited book to completion." After some attempts, and failures, you will eventually get a name and publishers will contact you. At first, but also constantly during your career, we have predatory and vanity publishing. But then more respected publishers, most likely commercial ones, will also ask you to publish with them. They need you. You have a name, and status, making them claim that you say things that make sense and are useful. They will help you market your name to "become famous" and will make money in exchange for this. This is a win-win situation for you both but not for taxpayers and for academics with poor libraries, who cannot afford your books—and we are not talking about a minor fraction of libraries in the world.

I once asked a commercial editor, now a good acquaintance of mine, after several books were published with them, "How much money would you need me or my university to pay if I want that my book comes out with you immediately in paperback without having it published in hardcover first, and obviously being sold solely at the hardcover price?" I understood that they had to see a profit and was not against that, I simply wanted my book to be accessible to more people, while being able to associate my name with that very publisher, which I needed at that time. His answer was honest but frightening. He said, "I have a moral problem here, I cannot ask an academic to pay whatever €10.000 to subsidize a book knowing that top managers in my company are making €100–150.000 a year on your work already."

Can we reverse this trend? As anyone who has been in the academic sector long enough knows, academia is an extremely conservative environment. The quasi-monopoly of commercial publishers has been challenged by some independent, and sometimes radical, publishers. However, they are not large enough to gain the attention from a majority of universities, and ministries, that keep relying on more standard, and conservative, classifications and quality control mechanisms.

I think, for instance, of many countries in Central and Eastern Europe who, only after titanic efforts, have been able to create a quality control mechanism based on the major databases and publishers (Scopus, Web of Science). How can you go to them and say, "It is all so nice of you, but once you have finally agreed on quality standards, please start a new commission to do a classification of open source, and non-Scopus-indexed, publishers?"

Academics seem happy to work for free to pay for other people's salaries and then complain that they do not make enough money. This is not the only case. It emerged some years ago that UK academic salaries for junior staff were being cut while salaries for administrative staff was being increased beyond limits. In principle, that is understandable. If I need a person capable to earn the university several millions per year, I need to buy out this person from the private sector and thus attract them with equivalent benefits, prestige and money. But we are not far from the situation of a factory worker earning 10% of what their top manager earns. Why do we stubbornly look at the academic sector as public? Corporate logic is widespread already and big money is there. Just think of the demand for Western education and how it has been growing in the past years. And what should I answer when a colleague says that they would like to attend a conference, but they cannot because their university would not subsidize €500 for it...after all, there is not much money in academia. Right?

What if you have no money to go to a conference?

Ok, so you are one of those who have been denied the €500 and cannot go to an international event. What to do? Well, there is never enough money, we know this, but what is the real meaning of "there is no money?"

The main problem I have with the "no money" statement is that, at least in most cases I hear it, it sounds like there is no money falling from the sky for that conference. But how much does "a conference" cost? Big conferences cost a lot, there are debates about them being elitist and excluding most scientists and I would tend to agree. On the other side of the spectrum, there are e-conferences, where you can present via VOIP protocols. I see a conference as a chance to meet colleagues, both in a formal and informal setting so that just presenting via the internet you miss out on "most of the fun" that includes networking possibilities. My assumption is, thus, that if you attend a conference, you want to be there physically but if you really need to go there this is an option.

How hard is that if you cannot secure support from your department? During my PhD years, I had no institutional support, or even a PhD scholarship, but I attended several conferences. Sometimes I would get some sporadic, and limited, travel grants but most of the time I would just pick the ones where I could go on a minimal budget. Of course, I could not go to conferences in the US or New Zealand. But, during fieldwork in Ukraine, I could attend conferences in Poland or Ukraine itself. I once saw a good opportunity in Kaunas and went there by bus. It took a while, but I see it this way: if you have no time, invest money to get there quickly; but if you have no money, then invest in time and you will be able to go there on a low budget. Once at the conference, I took advantage of social networks (like hospitality club at that time) to find someone who could host me for free somewhere. I thus compensated lack of money with creativity and time spent finding alternatives.

What if I live faraway or in an isolated country and cannot travel?

There are several levels of isolation. This question arose by someone from Armenia that is in a particularly difficult situation. Borders with Turkey and

Azerbaijan are virtually closed, the border with Iran is open but far from any major cities so that the only easily crossable border is with Georgia.

I think that the main limit to attending conferences (and to travel in general) is our fantasy, or knowledge at best. There are several conferences that you can attend with little or no money. First, there are the conferences in your own country. Travel is affordable, and the level of the conference might be better than you think. Do not think of only nationally organized ones, think of international projects that want to hold a conference in the region. In many cases, they are easier and cheaper to organize than conferences at your home university. Local universities are happy to help with work, provide rooms and catering is likely to be cheaper.

At the end of the day, in my view, information is worth more than money. Learning about a conference in your country, or even your city, where you have high-level scholars coming is priceless. I appreciate that it is always difficult to get rid of your routine in the place where you live, that you will be receiving hundreds of calls about daily issues during the conference. However, if you want to make time and space for someone, or something, you are able to do it. It is a matter of priorities and attitudes. Silence your phone as you would do it at a conference abroad. Tell people that you are unavailable that particular day and you have created the "abroad" setting allowing you to attend a conference at home as you would do elsewhere.

What I see as another limit is the fact that we are used to thinking "international conference equals travel," which is one of the perks of academia nowadays. This means that we get frustrated if other people travel and we do not. In my view, the advantage of an international conference is the chance to meet good scholars from other universities. It is nicer to do this in a hotel on some exotic beach but, with little money available, the location of a conference should be a secondary concern.

There might be large and important conferences in your country. At the end of the day, international conferences have an interest in rotating locations to become more attractive but also the share the burden of organizing, to give more universities the chance to become visible. If you live in a high-income country, it is statistically easier to find money to go. But if you are based in a low-income country, you might not have money to go to conferences, but you are in a good position to attract international conferences. Food, venue and social activities are much cheaper than in a high-income country. After all, you could even consider finding a team and offering to host an international event at your university. It is tiring but you will definitely be able to attend an international conference. You will also be able to claim credit for the organization of an international event.

What if there is nothing in my country and I need to present at an international event?

Travel nowadays is easier. Within the EU but also in many other world regions there are many low-cost airlines that, properly handled, can take you there and back for €100. In other cases, such as the former USSR spaces, trains are an excellent alternative and can take you virtually everywhere. For some routes, coach companies offer some decent options. From Chisinau you can easily enter Ukraine or Romania, Minsk is relatively near the Baltics and Poland, in addition to Russia. Not all locations offer the same opportunities. From Baku or Yerevan, the only easy destination is Tbilisi. However, I would say that Georgia is a major international hub since anyone doing research in the region goes there to have an easier life than in its neighboring countries. From Georgia there are also several decent travel options to its neighbor Turkey but also to a number of other places. It is a matter of searching for a good combination and activating your fantasy.

Another possible way is to coordinate your stay is with your holiday. If you always wanted to go to Paris and you find out that a good conference will be hosted there at a time when you can go, then you can arrange to do both things. True that your partner, if you promised to go with them, might not be as enthusiastic about this but it is also true that if you do not do it all the time, they can show some sympathy for your cause and agree to spend 2–3 days separate and then stay longer to do what tourists want to do.

Still, there are travel grants offered by conference organizers and you could always try. But try to think beyond the paradigm "if I do not win any money, then I will not go" since then you might remain home for a long period of time. Also, try to avoid applying blindly for all available travel grants or you might spoil your reputation. For one thing, if I announce a conference on urban studies and someone in the field of EU foreign policy applies, or even asks if there is money for their travel available, I will suspect that they are more interested in the location, or free travel, than in the conference itself.

I might then make a mental note about the person, a thing that might make me look at them with suspicion in the future, even if the conference is on a topic they actually focus on.

The problem, in my view, is more a lack of information, or creativity, than a lack of money. There are a few conferences where most people assume they have to go. You learn about them and dream to go there. But you do not look at what is happening in other places nearby you, where there might be a major conference of which you are not aware of. If you have no money, then invest the time into searching on the Internet, identify colleagues to work with, the larger your network the more likely to be invited to international conferences. Information gathering that will allow you, in the long term, to identify perhaps better opportunities for your career you were not aware of before. You might also want to go "off the beaten track," where there are fewer people to compete with and possibly more money is available. English is widely accepted as the language for scientific communication in a great majority of countries. Still, I also know that some colleagues from the post-Soviet region, who can speak German or at least work with German universities, get regular invitations and are offered for their expenses to be paid when they go and present their joint project. Scandinavian countries also have, on average, more funding then other places in the world so if you cannot compete on the EU or US market it may pay to explore alternative places.

Going to an international conference is not easy but is not impossible either. You should ask yourself: where can I possibly go with the budget I have? You might be based in relatively isolated locations with visas and border limitations. But international does not necessarily mean to go far away. I once heard a director encouraging his staff to go from Germany to Austria if they still wanted to present in German. At least Austria could be considered "abroad," and they could claim to be going to an international conference.

What is a deadline and what is an academic deadline?

I often see colleagues stressing because they need to submit an article, or chapter, "by tomorrow." Some might work all night because they need to submit a piece "by the deadline." But what is a deadline? And what is an academic deadline? And why am asking this question in the funding section?

I see deadlines belonging to two categories: imperative and not. Funding deadlines are, in most cases, non-negotiable. They are decided by relatively large organizations with a complex bureaucratic structure where decisions are made by a board and cannot be changed easily. The capacity to move a deadline depends on that before whom an organization is responsible. If I am managing public funds, I will have a lot of pressure to keep things transparent and fair. This means to show that I am acting according to some protocol and I am not preferring or penalizing anyone. If a large donor like the European Commission has no applicants, it is unlikely that re-advertisement will be possible. If a large donor states that the deadline is at 17:00, there is no way to extend this.

If I am managing no private funds (mine or of a private donor), it becomes easier to juggle a deadline. Think of re-advertisements or extended deadlines for a position or a contribution. If I do not have any applicants or not sufficiently qualified applicants, I can extend the deadline if I am in the department. I might just need some sort of internal agreement. Even some private, or smaller, donors might allow a certain level of flexibility and permit you to submit some extra documents few days after the deadline

If there is such elasticity when dealing with funds, thus high interests, I would guess that all other situations should be easier to deal with. I am not talking only of the case where no money or high interests are involved. I am also thinking of situations where an individual, or a small team, can make decisions alone and with no constraints from a higher authority.

Deadlines for abstracts, articles, chapters are, most likely, at the discretion of a single person or a very restricted group of scholars. This means that if we have an agreement that you will submit your chapter by the 25th of this month, it is very unlikely that on the 26th I need to send the whole manuscript. It is also very unlikely that I know when I will be sending the manuscript. I often joke that in academia there are no deadlines. Well, that is not really a joke and I have rarely encountered an imperative deadline in academia. Think in terms of probability. What are the odds that, if I am awaiting 12 abstracts or, worse, 12 chapters, everyone will submit them on the agreed deadline? Not only might have I agreed on different times with different people depending on their schedule (and at different times of the year); it is also very unlikely that everyone will jostle their other commitments to submit exactly when they have to.

I consider an academic deadline for a book, or similar things, a period of 2–3 months over which most—and hopefully all—authors will send me their work. This means, at least to me, that if you are 2–3 days late there is not even a need to inform the editor (and I mean even if I am the editor, I do not care, or will not even notice, if you are 2–3 days late). You need to formally inform him if you are going to be 10–15 days later and you need to negotiate if you want even more time. But there is no need to have a sleepless night just before the deadline since the chances that someone will read your work as you send it are very low.

I am aware that there are colleagues much stricter with time, and serious, if you want. But I hope, with these examples, to reduce the level of stress some of us have before a submission. If you are applying for a €1M, then you have no choice but to stress out and lose your sleep. But if you are submitting a paper, chances are that the deadline is negotiable not once but several times.

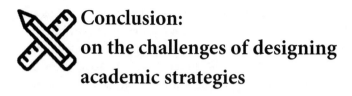# Conclusion:
on the challenges of designing
academic strategies

...Conclusion? There is no conclusion in strategy. Just as there is no time when you (can) stop thinking. If not only about your job. You think about what the fastest way home is, the best quality-price ratio at a supermarket, how to escape that dinner to which you are invited to but have no desire to go to. At work, we think about how to develop a given idea into a paper, or a book, for a conference presentation, on whether to invest in going to this event or that one.

Our mind is constantly occupied, and preoccupied, by strategic reasoning, no matter whether we realize it or not. So, there is no way to get it to an end, find the perfect recipe and go on with your life. Just as much as there is no perfect, final or definitive choice. There is no "right" or "wrong" choice either. Better or worse is contextual, not absolute.

I once applied for a job and received no answer for some weeks. I then wrote to the head of the selection committee saying, "I understand you might have found a better candidate for the position." I liked his reply a lot, "We have not found a better candidate, we have found a candidate that suits us better in this given moment." Better and worse are not only subjective but subject to the time dimension. What is better for you at a given time is not necessarily better after some weeks, or years.

I decided to add a conclusion to this book after receiving 7 rejection letters in 3 months. Basically, all the grants I applied for were rejected. Can I say that I failed? Is it the end of my fundraising success story? Is it the end of Abel as a strategist? It is not. Just inasmuch as winning another project or making another "good decision" would not make me a better strategist or fundraiser. Surely, winning a couple of millions would increase my value on the market (and my self-esteem) for some time. But my value would decrease as soon as someone else wins more than I do in a given moment.

Strategy, as I see it, is not about making the good choice(s) or winning all the time. Strategy is about thinking of possible ways you can continue doing what you want, or like, to do, by calculating your risks and eventually make choices that suit you at a given time. You do not need to be successful to be rich and do not need to be rich to be happy. Different people have different needs, ways of measuring things, skills, and ambitions. Someone's ultimate desire may be to spend hours in a library working on their manuscript. Someone else might dream of being famous, to write a book that everybody eventually reads and discusses. Some other people might dream of leaving the academic sector or not being put under pressure to do research since they simply like teaching and having contact with students. What you want at a given stage in your career is not necessarily what is asked for, or required, from you. In the corporate sector, it is somehow easier since people state, at least initially, that they want to have money. In the end, they also want other things, but often money is prioritized and may be regarded as the common denominator.

Ultimately, we all need money, to various extents. However, I find it difficult to think that people from the academic sector put money as a first priority. Or they would not strive to get an academic job that gives, in most cases, so little money after so many years of study and training. So, what do you want?

What your employer wants is clear. They want simply everything from you: please teach, do research, administration, public engagement, fundraising, publications (possibly in a top journal, but top journals are top because not everyone gets into them), get a Nobel prize, present at the best conferences (possibly without asking for money from the department), attract money from the business sector and more. But how much can you give? How many hours are you ready to spend working per day or per week? How many hours can you work before completely burning out? And what can you offer your employer without compromising your health, family, personal ambitions so to leave your strengths for other things that you like?

This is the meaning of strategy I use in this book: finding a compromise between what you are requested to do and what you want to do; take risks and work unpaid because you feel this is bringing you something; fail and fail again, possibly because this is the only way to understand what is really worth working and investing your time in. But, by doing all of this, feel that you are doing what you like to do at a given stage of your life or career. If you feel that you are squeezed by so many things that you need to do and lose your focus then have no time to do what you actually like to do, then perhaps you need to rethink your strategy.

This was the secret (even to me) idea behind the Scopus diaries. I have invested time and effort in many things, some of which have led me far while some others nowhere. But I could not know what it was worth until I tried them out. I have worked many times for free, for little money, knowing that money would eventually come and that I was being paid in other ways (experience, company of nice people, travels, food or food for thought). I sometimes have spent some extra time working, even if I had to sacrifice other things, to reach the conclusion that it was not worth it. But now I know it from experience and I will not feel guilty that I am late with a paper or with a task because I know that to deliver on time would mean to sacrifice things that I do not want to sacrifice. I also know what a priority is, and I cannot be late with (i.e., a funding deadline), and what can wait for me (i.e., a submission of this book manuscript, that I have delayed several times). I am not proud of being late and I try to warn people, or I try not to take up too many things. But I am also aware that the most important person I should not let down is myself. To do this, I have to think all the time of a strategy to compromise between what I feel I need and what I am required to do. I also know that I might miscalculate or misunderstand something. But in that case, the only solution is to be humble enough to stop, admit your mistake and rethink your strategy. Or your life. This also sometimes happens.

Naples, September 2018